Rolf Hochhuth
# MOZART'S NACHTMUSIK
Requiem for three characters in two scenes
adapted by
Robert David MacDonald

OBERON BOOKS
LONDON

Originally published under the title *Nachtmusik*.

Copyright © 2000 Rowohlt Velag GmbH, Reinbek bei Hamburg.

This translation first published in 2001 by Oberon Books Ltd. (incorporating Absolute Classics)
521 Caledonian Road, London N7 9RH
Tel: 020 7607 3637 / Fax: 020 7607 3629

e-mail: oberon.books@btinternet.com

Copyright © translation and adaptation Robert David MacDonald 2001

Rolf Hochhuth is hereby identified as author of *Nachtmusik*, in accordance with section 77 of the Copyright, Designs and Patents Act 1988. The author has asserted his moral rights.

Robert David MacDonald is hereby identified as author of this adaptation in accordance with section 77 of the Copyright, Designs and Patents Act 1988. The author has asserted his moral rights.

A catalogue record for this book is available from the British Library.

ISBN: 1 84002 259 0

Cover design: Oberon Books

# Characters

FRANZ HOFDEMEL
aged thirty-six

MAGDALENA HOFDEMEL
his wife

EMPEROR LEOPOLD II
aged forty-three

*Eine Kleine NachtMusik* was first performed by the Citizens' Company at the Citizens' Theatre, Glasgow, on 25 October 2001, with the following cast:

FRANZ,  Edward Hooper

MAGDALENA,  Anne-Marie Timoney

LEOPOLD,  Tristram Wymark


Director,  Robert David Macdonald

Designer,  Philip Witcomb


Scene 1

A living-room in the
Gruenangergasse, Vienna

Scene 2

The small music-room in
the Hofburg Palace, Vienna

'During the several months I spent in Vienna in 1852, I spoke on numerous occasions with Carl Czerny, who, in his amiable, forthcoming way, told me many interesting things about Beethoven, based on his years of acquaintance with him. One day, when he had described to me several things about his extraordinary powers of improvisation, he added that Frau Hofdemel as well, the pupil and friend of Mozart, had declared, after hearing Beethoven, that he had surpassed Mozart. It had, in fact, been no easy matter for her to get Beethoven to play something for her. She had come to Vienna on a visit, and had lodged with Czerny's parents, and, on her expressing the urgent wish to hear Beethoven, Czerny's father had gone with his son, who, as a young man, was enjoying Beethoven's teaching, to see Beethoven, and reported Frau Hofdemel's entreaty. "Hofdemel?" asked Beethoven, "Isn't that the woman who had that business with Mozart?", and on receiving an affirmative answer, declared roundly that he would not play for that woman, and that it was only later, after considerable persuasions, that he could be brought to let the woman visit him, at which meeting he did improvise.

'To my question about what the "business with Mozart" would have been, Czerny expressed astonishment, that it was unknown to me, and told me that Frau Hofdemel had been the pupil of Mozart, and that her husband had become jealous of him, and in a fit of rage attempted to murder his wife, only succeeding in wounding her severely with slashes across the throat and the breast, and then killed himself. He, Czerny, had himself seen the woman, who lived in Bruenn, on several occasions in his youth, when visiting his family home, and since he had noticed how she had attempted to hide the terrible scars on her neck with a scarf tied in a particular way, the matter had been explained to him by his father.

'As Czerny saw how the story took hold of me, he expressed, in some fearfulness, his wish not to be named as the authority for it, and assured me that in early years, it had been general knowledge in Vienna.'

Otto Jahn: *Collected Essays on Music*, Leipzig 1866

'One can say everything, since the most intimate detail is the most widespread.'

Otto Flake, 1976

About 5.30 p.m. on the sixth December 1792.

This date is important, as marking the day after Mozart's death and the day of his burial, since the pioneer biographer Otto Jahn, 'with genuine relief', cut the whole Hofdemel tragedy out of the second edition of his Mozart biography, because he fell into the trap of accepting the doubtless intentionally falsified date of death of Franz Hofdemel, and, in his Mozart-Supplement of 1863 – in book form 1866 – asserted the utterly absurd statement that Hofdemel committed suicide not on the day of Mozart's burial, but not until four days afterwards.

However, on the third of May 1971, Dr Felix Czeike, Senior Archivist of the City and the Province of Vienna, under the document MA 67 – 106/71, informed the present author: '1. In the death registrations of the city of Vienna, sixth of December 1791, Franz Hofdemel was registered as dead (i.e. not five days after Mozart's death). The entry which refers to the death as suicide, runs: "Hofdemel Franz, Senior Clerk of the High Court of Justice, who took his own life in his residence at 1360 Rolleterisches Haus in the Gruenangeergasses, and who was judicially examined in the General Hospital, was thirty-six years of age. Sortori, Senior Surgeon. (Registration of deaths 1791, letter H, fol. 80; the address corresponds to the present-day address at Vienna 1, Gruenangergasse 10.)"' In the same letter, Archivist Czeike indicates how the falsifying and disappearance of the Hofdemel tragedy doubtless only took place because of its connection with the tragedy of the Mozarts, why else? He continues: '2. At the end of the eighteenth century, the only newspaper existing in practice in Vienna was the Wienerische Diarium, the forerunner of today's Wiener Zeitung, founded under this name in 1803. A thorough examination of the issues in the weeks after Mozart's death until the end of the year 1791 gives no sort of indication or mention of the murder attempt or of the suicide of Hofdemel; even the death of Hofdemel recorded in the registration of deaths, is not picked up in any of the regular columns of deaths appearing in Vienna.'

Why was the death of a respected court official suppressed even in 'the regular columns of deaths appearing in Vienna'?

# Scene 1

*The living-room in the Gruenangergasse in Vienna, where the Hofdemels were accustomed to give chamber concerts. A spinet, a cello, and the three violins that Hofdemel possessed. Eight, if possible twelve chairs, and four stools; stood up against the wall, as normally in the eighteenth century. Two white-gold mirrors, beneath them two-legged rococo console tables. A portrait of MAGDALENA, by the best pupil of Liotard; following the pattern of Liotard's 'Girl Reading' in the Dresden Gallery. Liotard, from Geneva,, who also did portraits of all sixteen children of Maria Teresia, was the most celebrated pastel portraitist in history. There is also a large landscape in the manner of the French seventeenth century. Left and right are large doors, not double doors, but tall. Before MAGDALENA enters, we hear, then later see FRANZ HOFDEMEL at his cello: Boccherini – the latest composition of King William II of Prussia's Court Composer.*

*MAGDALENA enters, in mourning: she wears a strikingly large three-cornered hat, differentiated from a man's only by a lanyard hanging down at the back and by a deep black veil, worn with an elegant, knee-length cape – black of course.*

MAGDALENA: (*Who has entered from the right of the stage, and is taking off her gloves.*)
Aha! Making music! Where is Therese?

FRANZ: You took the child over to the neighbours' yourself.

MAGDALENA: Yes, right up to the end I gave you credit for being clever enough to come with me!

FRANZ: Clever. Does one go to a funeral out of cleverness?

MAGDALENA: In your case, yes.

*She starts taking off her heavy, fairly high-heeled shoes, which she is wearing in December, although on that afternoon, contrary to the reports falsified for posterity, the weather was 'mild, with widespread mist' as Francis Carr quotes from Count Zinzendorf's diary, adding that 'the official barometer readings and the general weather forecast confirm this*

*statement'. Who invented the tale of a thunderstorm storm?
Why should such a story have been contrived? Clearly to explain
the disappearance of the body into anonymity.*

*FRANZ makes no move to help his wife out of her cape. He
goes on playing, but only broken-off phrases. Her hat she will
take off later.*

*She is still busy removing her shoes; then to the next room or
to the wardrobe, where she hangs her cape, and hat, and puts
her shoes, changing them for a pair of elegant house shoes, not
slippers.*

Not that your hatred is wiped out by his death;
but you should have had the sense to know
there would be talk, if you didn't go.

FRANZ: Talk! Even if I *had* gone there.

MAGDALENA: You were lucky.
There was too much going on, without
there being time to chatter about us as well.
*Constanze* was not there!

FRANZ: Quite right too. Can't death even put
an end to all that hypocrisy?

MAGDALENA: At least I was spared that…and
Mozart was spared it too,
her playing the widow and in public!
But everyone, everyone who was allowed to see him, at
the end –
Sophie says –
he was so swollen, it could only have been poison.
It was agreed between the two doctors
there was not to be an autopsy,
nor were they to write a report.
Just a death-mask – masks don't say anything –
one was taken.

FRANZ: Who was the second, the second doctor?

MAGDALENA: Doctor von Sallaba.
Dr Closset was at the theatre, and *stayed* in the theatre
as the theatre doctor – but then came too early,
when Sophie had run to fetch him.
Then came the vinegar poultice, which he prepared,
*That* made Mozart unconscious!
Finally. Up till then he'd gone one working at the Requiem.
Everything I know I have from Sophie, who,
at least when Constanze's not there, talks to me normally.

*FRANZ, as if in triumph, holds up the 'Wiener Zeitung',
unaware that, according to Francis Carr's researches, it is
only in the provincial press, and never in the Viennese, that
he and his wife will be written about the next day and the
day after...he holds the paper – tabloid format in the eighteenth
century – so that the banner cannot be read.*

FRANZ: But on whose order is it that there's still not a word
in the paper, not one single syllable – ! Nix.
Died in the night of the fourth to the fifth,
I went out specially this morning to get the paper
when he was already buried –
nothing in the paper even on the sixth,
not a single word!
One of yesterday's great men of course
– yesterday's anyway!

MAGDALENA: (*Laughing contemptuously.*)
Yesterday? You stupid, envious sheep!
Not three months since the premiere of Magic Flute!

FRANZ: Even so: can only be orders from the palace
not to write anything.

MAGDALENA: The palace? Why?
The Emperor had nothing against him. The church, yes!
But what newspaper still obeys the Church?
Of course, when Sophie ran to fetch a priest, the Church
sent nobody until the last moment, when it was too late –
Mozart was already unconscious from the vinegar compress.

'To that bad a Catholic we do not come,'
said one of the barbarians of St. Stephan,
as Sophie calls the black brothers.

FRANZ: (*With almost the same grimace as before.*)
You think, you really imagine, they knew nothing
about you and him, about Suessmayer and Constanze.
you four it was fucked his chances, literally, of being buried
like Gluck three years ago…all right, he was no Gluck,
not by a long chalk, in his own opinion at very best.
But getting rid of him like a dog,
he was not that much worse than Gluck!
No obituary, no word the next day in the paper,
however not…?
It can only have been on the orders of All-Highest!

MAGDALENA: It'll be in tomorrow, the obituary.
There was someone there from the paper.
I'm glad he didn't get anything in today,
then he'd be able to report tomorrow morning
that Constanze didn't even buy a grave for her husband.

*But the paper will not write a syllable about the unworthy
disposal of the corpse, although they brought an announcement
the following day, the 7.12.91: 'Already known since childhood,
throughout Europe for the rarest musical talent, by the most
fortunate development of his excellent gifts of nature…achieved
the stature of the greatest masters…' A Berlin newspaper
mentioned that Mozart had been poisoned.*

FRANZ: Why should she have, for your bit of trade,
a grave for *him*? How can you, of all people, expect that?

MAGDALENA: But the same barbarians –
just like you're one of them –
the ones who didn't send a priest on time,
they kept quiet on purpose about
where the last leavetaking was to be, so quickly,
that no one came, because they didn't know,
and not even in the cathedral, just at the side chapel,

where the steps go down into the crypt.
And then, brought out of sight, the body.
At least Sophie and I and Joseph Deiner
went out with it.

FRANZ: (*With a satisfaction he cannot hide.*)
And where is his grave?

MAGDALENA: Not in the main cemetery,
but where no one will see it –
three miles away from the cathedral,
in the St. Marxer cemetery.

FRANZ: (*Shouting with satisfaction.*)
The Marxer – which is hardly still in Vienna!
Tell me, do they still bury people that far out?

MAGDALENA: That's why I'm so late coming home.

*Dejected and ashamed, with the feeling that she should have
done something to stop the unworthy ceremony, which she
naturally had no power to do.*

I wanted to know, even if I couldn't believe it,
that that godless Constanze allowed…
At least she had enough shame, not to come along.
There was only me, Sophie and me, and a woman
I didn't know, just the three of us women and…

FRANZ: Oh yes, just like for our lord Jesus.
With Mozart like with our Saviour:
three women, among them – whyever not, of course,
a Mary Magdalen, you, his whore *en titre!*

*She slaps him with the back of her hand – she is still wearing
long gloves – in his grinning face, when he has barely uttered
this – albeit matter-of-fact – comparison.*

MAGDALENA: I his whore – yes!
His last, single happiness!
You – his poisoner!

FRANZ: That's why you wanted me to have been there:
    you'd read somewhere
    like everybody else, a murderer always returns to the body,
    if he can't return to the scene of the crime!
    It was supposed to overcome me, my going with you.
    But in the side chapel – the size of a hatbox –
    were there at least enough people there?

MAGDALENA: More than there will be when you go.
    And even though it had been purposely prevented
    from anybody finding out by looking in the paper,
    where the leavetaking was happening.
    and so that no one would be able to go along –
    that far out, where practically no one is buried any more.
    That Constanze should have allowed,
    that he should not have had a grave at all,
    but just be put with other people in a row!

FRANZ: (*Stops his grinning, almost as if he now was sorry for
    his victim.*)
    No grave? – just in a row like a pauper?
    But Mozart wasn't *poor!*
    Even that last loan he had from me
    for the journey to Berlin: he paid it back on the nail!

MAGDALENA: (*Irritated.*) Why ever not? He always did.
    He forced my father to take his heavy gold watch,
    worth ten times the little loan he had to ask for
    in Bruenn, on his way back from Prague.
    Constanze had only gone with him at the price
    of being allowed to take her Suessmayr to Prague with her.
    Because he knew he was being poisoned,
    Mozart *forced* my father to accept his watch –
    because he knew, he would not be in a position
    to pay that small loan back again!

FRANZ: His body not in a grave – but with the paupers?
    Then they must know something!
    It's on orders from the Palace…it must be.

MAGDALENA: I told you: two doctors witnessed to it,
that he was swollen up as if he'd been poisoned.
And Sophie couldn't understand either, how Baron Swieten,
who admittedly stayed behind in the side chapel
like everyone else, apart from us three woman and your
                                               Joseph –
but Swieten had ordered a good normal grave
for eight gulden, Sophie told me. But Mozart did not
come into that grave which Swieten had ordered for him!
He didn't come into it. Your Joseph promised me
he would go to Constanze tomorrow and tell her,
(but she will do nothing)
that no one will be able to find Mozart,
if she does not immediately put up
at least to start with, a wooden cross... I shall do so
today is Tuesday, if there is still not one there
next week. And I shall go tomorrow to Count Deym,
for him to sell me a cast of the death-mask
which – Sophie says – he took in the death-house
with plaster of Paris, for his waxwork collection.
Yes, plaster of Paris, Sophie said,
so why do they call them waxworks, not plaster works?

FRANZ: *You* will put up no cross, *you* will not bring his
                                               death-mask
into my house, true as my name's Franz Hofdemel,
who he put horns on a hundred times,
sixteen pointed antlers,
who Mozart only called his friend
when he was pumping money out of him!

MAGDALENA: How revolting, your being at home now.
I would never have come back, if I had known.
I wanted – as he had begged me, his last words to me:
'Play the Requiem, as far as it's ready,
when you come back from burying me.'
I wrote down every day what he had done.
But I don't need to play it,

it's playing all the time inside me, I can even hear
what he is saying, calling out to various passages!
I'd never have come home
if I had not been sure, you were still at the office.

*What Mozart said, we do not hear, but the Requiem we do.*
*As soon as MAGDALENA began to talk of it, she hears it,*
*and so do we, just as, later on, as soon as she mentions the*
*Piano Concerto K.595, (probably) dedicated to her. FRANZ,*
*naturally, hears nothing.*

*MAGDALENA speaks more to herself than to him; he answers*
*violently in the middle of the quiet music, which by now –*
*despite long pauses – will have become an integral part of the*
*play, also in the other scene, since the Emperor Leopold was,*
*equally, a practising musician…*

Also to spare you the necessity
of meeting me here.

FRANZ: A necessity you would have been spared too,
but it is you
I do not wish to spare anything more,
and that includes the truth:
the truth that you alone are to blame for his death!
If you had not been fucking him for the last two years
– he would still be alive,
and court Composer to the King of Prussia!
And by the way, it was your showing off,
about fat Wilhelm trying to lure Mozart to Potsdam
with the salary of an archbishop,
first put me onto the fact
the two of you were involved, so to speak,
in your undercover pranks.

MAGDALENA: (*Contemptuously.*)
That is exactly what they were not.
We were hardly ever together under any kind of cover.
I was never able to spend a whole night with him.
And when we were together by day

everything was too violent, too happy too, for any cover
not to have fallen off the bed, but of course, you

*She speaks in an insultingly pitying tone.*

would never understand that, how could you?
Quite apart from that, he, unlike you, had
a beautiful body, and I wanted to watch it all the time!
Not another word, that was just to pay you back
for your final admission that you poisoned him!

FRANZ: That I did.
But I confessed nothing, try and prove
I was that stupid, to say it to you,
of all people, to you, his whore!

MAGDALENA: That I don't need to claim,
enough people know, starting with Constanze,
he said – and how often towards the end, how often! –
'I know someone has given me Aqua Toffana.'
And that's why Sophie says the doctors decided…
No postmortem, no bulletins.
He knew: *you* were his murderer! Nobody else –
nobody had a motive.

FRANZ: But he didn't – first of all – didn't say it…

MAGDALENA: Oh, and how often, to me! And –

FRANZ: Yes, to you –
which, if you were wanting to blurt the whole thing out,
would only have proved you'd been his whore,
since why else would the Imperial Chancery Clerk
                                        Hofdemel
have given the composer poison, if not
because his wife –

MAGDALENA: (*Not without pride.*)
Wait and see. It's worth it to me
to be talked about by the whole world, as his lover,
all Vienna has known for ages

so long as it guarantees your being broken on the wheel
and executed: as his slayer…

FRANZ: (*Grinning.*)
You're so vain. Almost as vain as you are two-faced.
Dead men tell no tales.

MAGDALENA: There are enough witness, who heard him say
'I know, someone has given me poison.'

FRANZ: To be sure he did.
He said it four times in my very presence,
looking at me, as if I ought to fall down dead.
But he didn't say, '…and it was Franzi gave it to me'

MAGDALENA: How could he!
How could he have said *that*,
without giving me away to you and everyone else!
But it'll be proved after the exhumation!

FRANZ: (*With scorn.*)
What will? – oh, Aqua Toffana, to be sure. But with no
indication
of who gave it to him. And if you want an exhumation,
why did you dump him in a pauper's grave an hour and
a half ago
where – so soon – no one will be able to find him
among all the other rotting, decaying corpses!
I'll tell you why:
because you knew everybody would have thought it
simply foolish
to cut his body up
on account of such a nonsense, such twaddle!

MAGDALENA: That it is not nonsense has been proved
today,
since he was refused the grave von Swieten had already
ordered,
and simply got rid of in the row.
He said it often enough to enough people himself,

and now he has been put into a common ditch
no one will be dismissing it as nonsense,
above all when his corpse can prove it so clearly.
No one ever accused him of persecution mania!
And why dig him up? – the two doctors know why!
And Constanze knows why
and has stated that he had talked of it since June!
How long will it last, the promise
given to court flunkey von Swieten
not to issue any hospital bulletins!
Not every doctor loses a patient called Mozart,
who Posterity would show interest in.
At least one of those doctors is going to write up
what the future, in a hundred years, will be…

FRANZ: (*Laughs out loud, then, with scorn.*)
Future? – Mozart has barely still got a present.
Court Composer
and not even invited any more to write
the music for the last Imperial coronation.
How can you keep up this delusion for yourself
that in five years' time, a single person will
still know who your Wolfi ever was!

*With biting contempt.*

An 'immortal' like mein Herr Composer, cannot
of course, like the likes of us, be just put in a grave!
No, no – he has to have been poisoned at very least –
                                                dear God!
You said – he had no persecution mania.
Then call it his vanity.
He always looked sickly, timid,
jumpy as a goat.
Who would ever have taken him seriously enough
to find *that* necessary, to take the trouble
to give him poison.
His compositions show he was already written out,
a few measly themes – countless variations…

MAGDALENA: (*With crushing irony.*)
>There are a few, Franz, musicians among them,
>take the two of us, who still cannot quite
>make things in the way that Mozart could.
>Will you admit that? I mean to say!

FRANZ: The one who put on his 'Titus' in Prague
>apparently lost every penny!

MAGDALENA: (*Ignoring this.*)
>Since the world first began to turn, there have been
>how few? A dozen? – people who have
>become demigods: and one of them was Mozart!

*Her scorn strikes him speechless for a moment or two, then...*

FRANZ: Well, then, dig him up.
>No jumping to conclusions about the murderer allowed.

MAGDALENA: Just have to look at you, to know
>to *see:* you are a murderer. And my evidence
>will count!

FRANZ: With whom? With whom does it count what is said
>By a woman who has been able all these years
>To humbug her husband with such skill?

MAGDALENA: Then say that – then it will be your turn,
>then everybody will believe me, that it was you
>who – over and over – put Aqua Toffana into his drink.
>How often did you eat together!

FRANZ: A damned sight less often than you two had your
>>amusement
>With – how did you put it, his beautiful body?

*He gives her a sudden push, – which was meant to be a slap in the face, but missed – so strong that she falls.*

Liar! Infamous creature,
>who's going to believe another syllable from you,
>who've been deceiving your husband so consummately
>>all these years?

MAGDALENA: The truth is
    that I have not been deceiving you all these years.
    You knew about it, and even caught us very early on.

FRANZ: Yes, that one time – and was stupid enough
    To forgive you the same night. Not, be it said,
    from humanity, but in the certainty,
    the fear that all Vienna would laugh itself to death at me,
    if it knew it had been that pasty-faced thing,
    pale as a turnip, who had put such a pair of horns on me,
    so big I'd not be able to make it under the City gate – ha!
    That was the reason, the only one, but I hope
    a reasonable one. Why do most of those who know
    and most of them always do know! –
    that their husbands or wives are playing away,
    why do they look away and hold their tongues –
    they are *ashamed* like I was.
    They hold their tongues, so as not to be laughed at to death!
    the only reason. 'Only'? and quite enough too, I'd think.

MAGDALENA: (*Without irony, almost with affection,*
    *spontaneously.*)
    Ashamed? – you mustn't be that, Franz,
    You never had any sort of chance against him!
    any more than – believe me! – than I did: not a chance
    to say no to him.

FRANZ: (*Gloomily.*)
    Who believes that – nobody! No, I would have been,
    I *was* laughed at to death by everyone,
    everyone who knew. And who did not know?
    They even knew, with *whom* you
    had put horns on me. Who had done it.
    A clapped-out down-at-heel whose own wife
    had long since decamped to Baden-Baden with Suessmayr!
    How long is it now that Constanze dropped him,
    so as to have his – haha: *his!* – child, courtesy of
    Suessmayr, while he was still his pupil,
    when he didn't even yet have to shave!

MAGDALENA: (*Gives him a slap on the face strong enough to knock the glasses off his nose.*)
You sneer at him, he hasn't been in his grave
above two hours…

FRANZ: (*Laughs menacingly.*)
But you can't deny that his pupil
had to make his last child for him!

MAGDALENA: Dear God, and by this…this murderer
I have a daughter!
Who, by the way, by her very existence
protects you from being tortured and hanged.
How could I do that to the girl,
expose her, make her world-famous as the daughter
of the man who knew the most world-famous
the only one – of living composers
and poisoned him!

FRANZ: (*With satisfaction.*) Not living any longer, – is he?

MAGDALENA: The only reason,
only because of Theresa can you be sure
that I shall not turn you in,
that I don't move Heaven and earth to have you tortured.

FRANZ: Such big talk. The 'only' world-famous one.
Not Haydn? Not Salieri, who is a lot cleverer?
Ha – the 'only' one!
Your keeping quiet has nothing to do
with consideration for me, even for our Theresa.
The only reason you don't go to the police
is that they'd put you in a lunatic asylum.

MAGDALENA: What do you mean, they only have to
exhume him
and it would be proved!

FRANZ: Oh, sure, but we have already heard that, you're
getting boring.
Poisoned by whom exactly?
The one who was so sure of it?

If she didn't do it herself, how could she know about it?
who is going to believe, that your husband,
whom he has been putting horns on for years,
would confess such a thing as that,
and to the murdered man's mistress of all people!

MAGDALENA: And what possible motive could I have had?

FRANZ: The one that women often find for vengeance on a
man;
being rejected by him! Wounded pride,
I've noticed, can make you – murderous!

MAGDALENA: (*Proudly.*)
Rejected! In which case, why should he, as all Vienna knows,
apart from you, not have gone as Court Composer, to
Berlin?
He did not go, solely because
he would have lost me! I begged him,
he *must* go to Prussia, but he couldn't leave me.

FRANZI: Thank you, so you did stop him.

MAGDALENA: Accidentally, yes. Against my will, yes.
Not behind anybody's back.
I begged him, how often, implored him at the end
to leave me and go to Potsdam!

FRANZ: And because you couldn't give up fucking him,
he died in Vienna instead of going to fat Friedrich Wilhelm
and finally – finally! – making something of himself.

MAGDALENA: 'Something': as if he had been nothing
here all this time!

FRANZ: You know quite well he was no longer anything in
Vienna
but an honourable legend –
whose shining future was a good fifteen years behind him!

MAGDALENA: 'The Magic Flute'
is not a quarter of a year ago!

FRANZ: And taken off already,
    after how few performances?

*He suddenly slaps her in the face, so that she stumbles and
has to holds on to a chair to stay upright.*

And as for that oh so beautiful body,
even if I hadn't given the bastard a push in the right
                                direction,
he'd never have got to be as old as he looked already.
And so it was *your* crime to stop him going to Prussia!
Why else d' you think I lent him the hundred gulden
he asked me for as travel money to Potsdam?
So that he would finally be away from here.
And then – the last sentence of his begging letter –
his generous promise – 'there'll soon be an end to your
                                 business'.
Because he imagined his recommendation
would carry some weight with his lodge-brothers!
As if I wouldn't be accepted by the freemasons without him.
Quite witty though, that last sentence in his
last letter to me: 'there'll soon be an end to your business.'
No, my dear Mozart, yours, not mine, your business
was very near to its end…well, mine too. Yes.
As if his recommendation had not been the opposite
of one in Vienna for years…and it was not of such
                                 importance
to me to become the lodge-brother of my pandar-in-law…
as I must assume I had been for some time to the
                                 amusement
of the whole Residenz…cuckold-in-law.

*Repeats with unutterably unpleasant irony.*

'soon be an end to your business'…mine, ha!
Did he really have no idea, how near his business,
with you that is, was to its end… Oh, no, of course, we
                                 know
he not only had an idea, he knew quite well
and couldn't stop talking about it.

MAGDALENA: Has there ever, ever, been a murderer
    talk with such *pleasure* about his victim
    before he'd been two hours under the earth…
    it's unbearable, unbearable!

FRANZ: Victim? You should say 'rival', that would fit.
    Yes, rival. He takes my wife, I take his life.
    Where's the difference? At least, as a man of action, a thief,
    I could be on a level with what your loving gaze
    sees as a man world-famous,
    but who is an fact already forgotten.
    Funeral fourth-class; doesn't even get a gravestone.

MAGDALENA: He will – from me!

FRANZ: As true as I stand here: you will do no such thing!

MAGDALENA: (*Taking his tone.*)
    As true as I sit here – I shall!

    *FRANZ, with one pull, snatches the light chair from under
    her, and she falls on the carpet. He laughs like an idiot. She
    gets up and throws the little flower-vase from one of the
    console tables at him. It misses and smashes against the wall.
    But she only just missed…he is impressed.*

    Tomorrow I go to Bruenn – for good.
    I only came back anyway for one last time
    for Teresa's sake. But now I see
    I have to go now. I can't stay one more night
    in the same house as a murderer, the father of my daughter.
    I cannot. However, for Teresa's sake, I will
    help you cover up the fact that you are the murderer!

FRANZ: Your father will be pleased, if you
    go back to him – thrown out and without his granddaughter.
    Because I am not letting you take Teresa with you!

MAGDALENA: As if I was going to ask!

FRANZ: (*Quite changed, seriously, moved.*)
    Why must you take Theresa from me too?

MAGDALENA: So that she doesn't have to grow up with a
poisoner.

FRANZ: Adultery is also a crime.

MAGDALENA: There you go again –
as if you had never known.

FRANZ: As if that excused it. It only made it
the worse for me, knowing:
if I didn't kill him – it would last forever with you!
I only admitted it to you,
so you would *share* in my crime.
so you would have to say
*my* affair brought him to a mass grave, and always know, for
*my* sake the father of my daughter became a murderer.
And we can't go on like this either, Lena.

*He calls her by name for the first time. He has loved her
deeply, the twenty-three-year-old girl, as well-known in the
city for her beauty as admired for her talent as a pianist.*

For how can things continue with two people
who know something like that about each other?
It is a knowledge one cannot live with. Nor should one!
Should not live with, in the order of the world.

MAGDALENA: (*With scorn.*)
Order of the world! What a great order that is!
A madman – if I could persuade myself
that you were that – poisons, gives several doses of poison
to someone just for, I say just, for what is it compared to
death

just for sleeping with his wife!

FRANZ: (*Nods in agreement.*)
You're right, it won't do.
Going on living, and knowing the one thing that's
unbearable.

MAGDALENA: Ah, Franz, if that were true,
that you couldn't bear it,

it would show that you as a poisoner could at least still feel
a trace of conscience.

FRANZ: (*Laughs.*)
How we misunderstand each other – after so many years.
Yes, you misunderstand me. As you have for years!
I am not repentant for killing someone –
but for killing the wrong one:
him and not you. For how could he
have got away from you, I couldn't do it myself!
I have every sympathy, and more,
for the poor shrouded corpse, how could he
when I could not. Escape
from you, the Adriatic shipyard between your legs!
Pokorny!
What kind of name is that, you Czechs, you Slovaks,
you're all as good as Croats, Serbs, I don't know what.
He may have been your teacher – but even he
was not able to make you into a pianist!

MAGDALENA: (*Quite seriously.*)
Oh, am I not? I'm not a pianist?

FRANZ: At any rate, as you perfectly well know,
not one to be taken seriously in Vienna,
before you were Mozart's pupil, or rather, mistress,
as everybody, *everybody,* knew. He never had
a pupil, he didn't at once make a mistress of.
Perhaps at home, in Bruenn, where people take you seriously
because your name's Pokorny and your father
is the only musician there anyone's heard of,
perhaps you could make something of yourself.

MAGDALENA: (*Equally contemptuous.*)
I admit, if I were to give concerts not using the name
                                                    Pokorny
but as Magdalena Hofdemel,
people would laugh, but they wouldn't come.
Anyway, if I may remind you, as you've been good enough

to tell me nobody takes me seriously
has anyone ever taken you seriously? Well, who then?

FRANZ: I am a competent high clerk of the court of justice.
as such not without respect,
at any rate, the Emperor has often personally asked for me,
but unlike you, I do not pretend that what I do is art.

MAGDALENA: Never in all my life have I described myself
as an artist, because I never made art,
but merely passed on music that others had made – an
interpreter.
I don't go along with the new fashion, which says
the interpreter is more than the one who writes or
composes it!

FRANZ: But like all of them who just interpret
you wanted to write music.
When we were first married I used to catch you,
composing away, often, if you're honest…

MAGDALENA: I swear on Theresa's head,
I have not written a single note
since I became a pupil of – his.

FRANZ: Pupil – you mean mistress!
How long did it last then, before you became that,
one music lesson, or perhaps even two…?
You're like the woman in the old joke:
true to her husband right through the honeymoon…
Aha, not even that long, I have the feeling!

MAGDALENA: You said just now, *he* was the one you were
sorry for, having no chance,
sitting next to me at the keyboard,
Me the siren, the Croat.
Are you so insensitive, Franz, do you know so little
about love
you did not use to be like that – that you never ask yourself
how did I, the little piano player, escape from him?

But your stupid remark that no one took me seriously
as a pianist…you think he would have taken me on if…

FRANZ: Because he fancied you he took you on into the
                                                                bargain,
torturing himself next to you at the spinet.
It must have been a torment for him,
the man who wrote the Little Night Music
in a few hours, and…

MAGDALENA: (*Laughs, offended.*)
All the same, the pianist who nobody took seriously,
made enough money, so that quite often,
the Herr High Clerk of the Court of Justice
could put half his salary into the Savings Bank.
To the account of High Clerk Franz Hofdemel,
to which Frau Hofdemel did not have access…
Cheating old skinflint! Just goes to prove once again:
beware of those who you put under a debt of gratitude!

FRANZ: (*With an expansive bow almost down to the floor.*)
Thank you, thank you – for your contributions
to the household. Out of a guilty conscience
for having destroyed it, our household.

MAGDALENA: Guilty conscience, God knows!
But not on your account.
But because he, yes, I admit, turned down Potsdam for me.
And was murdered on my account.
Guilty conscience is just the beginning
I am destroyed each time I think of it –
yes, as you said, I brought him to his grave. Yes.
I want to go on living, but I cannot, since I know,
since I knew, he had to die by poison from my husband,
who gave it to him on my account…but Franz, when
I am dead, will you at least give Theresa to my sister?

FRANZ: At least?
As if Theresa wasn't everything I would have left.

MAGDALENA: Would you,
  since no one can believe a word you utter,
  would you make a legal declaration,
  that you will leave our child to my sister?

FRANZ: Why? She is very young.
  Your sister will have children of her own,
  and then ours is just a stepchild.
  Which of course does not worry you, people
  who imagine like you that they are 'living for Art…'

  *This last spoken with withering scorn, as if he were quoting
  an artistic nitwit.*

  Then all your nearest and dearest are no more to you
  than your stupid music books and instruments.

MAGDALENA: Have you concerned yourself more with
                                    the child than I have?
  Not so. I only came back from the burial, instead of
                                    killing myself,
  because I can't do that, before Theresa is in safety
  with my sister, safe from her father
  …Mozart's murderer. How could you do it?

FRANZ: Could I have gone on living, and *not* have done it?
  That apart, I was sure, even *your* lack of conscience
  would not go so far as to broadcast to the world,
  the father of your child, should, on your account
  however vain you are – have poisoned Mozart.
  I was sure, even you would not broadcast that to the world.
  And how do you know that I shall be here much longer?

MAGDALENA: (*Finally depressed.*)
  If it's true, what you say – that at any rate will be true
  that I not you, will have been to blame,
  for his being murdered,
  and so it must be me, not you, who has to leave.
  Because, Franz, for the two of us, sharing that one piece
                                    of knowledge,

there is no room any more on this earth.
How is one to live, knowing this?

FRANZ: (*Nods.*)
Yes, that is the one thing, our last agreement.
Lena, be good to me, let us kill ourselves together,
your father will fetch Theresa away to Bruenn.
I think together things would be easier, to finish off.

*Both are silent, finally he asks.*

One question, a last one – can you give me an honest
answer?
If not, rather leave it.

MAGDALENA: (*Completely worn down, and not without
sympathy for the fact that he is too.*)
What point would there be to any more cheating?

FRANZ: All right then, that one time, when neither of you
realised
I had come back home – already suspicious of course –
and was listening to you, before I broke in on you,
what did he mean about that with the virgin?

MAGDALENA: Virgin?

*She has immediately understood him: the question confuses
her so much that she has to support herself.*

Franz, I don't know what you're talking about.

FRANZ: (*Shouting, suddenly out of control.*)
What did he mean, I'm asking you.
He asked, and you both laughed a little;
'Are you still a virgin?'

MAGDALENA: (*Finally breaking out in shouts of the wildest
desperation.*)
Oh, Franz – leave it, this – what is the point of these…
*Details.* He is *dead!* He is rotting away, and
all through my, through your, through our fault!

FRANZ: (*Laughs, deathly sad, as he now speaks, calling her – as he seldom does – by name.*)
Yes, Lena, our last and only point of agreement:
that the two of us have killed him!
But if we must go down
as criminals and conspirators to all eternity…

MAGDALENA: I hope there is no such thing – as eternity.
It would be appalling
if death were not at least – nothing!
The end of all things – ach, the end, finish –
what a bless-ed idea!

FRANZ: Please, not generalisation, now!
What did he mean, what was that little laugh for,
with the question: 'Are you still a virgin?'

MAGDALENA: *Please*, Franz: not that – just not that, please, –
*I cannot talk now,*
understand me… later, perhaps, when…

FRANZ: (*Shouts.*) There's not going to be a later.
*Quiet:* For either of us! – no later. – no later.
But I finally want to know that. And only that!
'Are you still a virgin?'
I shall kill you, Lena,
if you don't tell me what he meant.

MAGDALENA: (*Shrugs.*)
Kill me then, better to save me the trouble.

FRANZ: Tell me. What did he mean?

MAGDALENA: (*Begging.*) Franz, just don't ask me that.
You know, just don't be so – so stupid!
You're a man, and not entirely unaware.

FRANZ: As I have nothing at all left to lose,
tell me – or I shall kill you, and then myself,
because this, and then not another thing

I want to hear from you…'are you still a virgin?'
And then your; 'Yes' – and both of you laughing quietly
and…

MAGDALENA: Leave it now – not that I'm frightened of you.
What else do you think still means anything to me in life?
There are tunes of his I can't get out of my head,
as if I had to convince myself, se's still alive,
alive for ever, ever, just because he
is under the earth…but you ask such stupid questions,
torment me with them.

*As she began to speak, the 'Masonic Funeral Music' comes in.*

FRANZ: Torments you! – you think nothing torments me?
And this question
which will not let me sleep, not for ages, with the two of
you laughing
in that cunning way – you call that question stupid?

MAGDALENA: And just that one?

FRANZ: Just that one, yes, for the life of me, haha, yes,
the life of me, I want to know:
'Are you still a virgin?'

*He has hauled her out of her armchair, and pulled her to him
as if he wanted to throttle her; perhaps he does.*

MAGDALENA: Spare yourself that, spare yourself the
answer!

FRANZ: I'm not sparing myself anything more, or you.
Why be sparing on the day you die!

*With which he throws her back in the armchair and dashes
out into the next room, returning equally fast, with an open
razor in his hand; the Masonic Music swelling a little.
Magdalena looks as if she now knew how the scene will end
– has to end. His expression is no longer 'of this world'.*

You tell me this minute
or I shall cut both our throats!

*He says this so quietly as to be believable.*

MAGDALENA: Yes, do that –
but first when Theresa is with my father.
Don't – just for a word – make our child an orphan
before she even gets to Bruenn.

FRANZ: The most intimate of your intimacies – they way
he laughed!
'Are you still a virgin' – it has made me mad
all these years… I have to know!

MAGDALENA: Franz, please – please not!

FRANZ: As if you still had a right to ask me for *anything*,
since destroying our life!

*Objective, cold, as having long considered the matter.*

On Theresa's account you need have no worries,
nor, on her account, should you have any hopes.
Yes, she will be better off with your sister than with us,
she is taken care of: I am a senior civil servant
and have nine thousand gulden put by…what did he,
apart from contempt for me – what did he mean by
'virgin'?

*He has the open razor at her throat again. With a deliberate
movement, she knocks it out of his hand, bends down quicker
than he, picks it up, and flings it right across the room.*

MAGDALENA: Contempt?
No, never, not with one syllable did he show that.
Quite on the contrary: he always said we could only do it
because he was taking nothing from you, but leaving me
with you…
Idiot – not to spare you – spare us that! 'Virgin'!
It was at the beginning, Franz,
when I still did it with you.

FRANZ: (*Tenses, as if she really had something else to reveal to him.*)
Still. Yes, sometimes. Seldom enough. Well?

MAGDALENA: (*Now very simply, concisely, shaking it off as it was self-evident, shrugs her shoulders.*)
He wanted to know, every time, it was a ritual between us, whether he could use his mouth on me.
Sixty-nine was not to be.
If there were still traces of you,
if I was not a virgin any more!

FRANZ: (*After a moment of threatening reflection.*)
Later – no, right away he wouldn't have needed to ask
any more.

MAGDALENA: Because you – only because you didn't
want to.

FRANZ: You would have done it with the two of us – gone on with both us?

MAGDALENA: Yes. Only the unimaginative say
you can only love one person.

FRANZ: Decent people – not unimaginative ones – say that.

MAGDALENA: Decent people, who also lack imagination.
And who are spared this perspicacity.
There is no merit in being unimaginative in love.
To be protected from – love. No merit, except when Love takes such a turn it brings one down to ruin.
The really great loved will always do that.
Look at the three of us!

FRANZ: But I would eventually have noticed it.
Since you did it…how did you choose to put it:
'every time' and as a ritual,
in other words time and again. *And again!*

MAGDALENA: You did not notice before,
not until the one time you caught us,
because he was holding back…

FRANZ: Ah – how moving, how respectful.

MAGDALENA: Not respect. We were circumspect.
Our fear you would find us out.
And his wanting, *always* to be wanting it.
I'm just telling you, because you will kill me,
tell one lie, do one murder… –
to tell you…there was no saving myself from him,
even if I had wanted to.

FRANZ: (*Devastated.*)
Intolerable…but no good to me,
no good at all to me, to have now the justification
for my action. It was,
tell me now with clarity, it was – necessary!

MAGDALENA: (*Shouts.*)
*Necessary!* Necessary, to kill him?

FRANZ: (*Making himself appear more cynical than he is, in his
certainty of being unable to live any more, because he has no
longer any wish to.*)
Let us say justified. He took my wife from me.
Years later, and after one has done *that*
having to see one's nearest, for whom one did it,
never even knew, who one was…

MAGDALENA:
What did you say: for whom one did it?
You must be utterly deranged now. You did it for me…?

FRANZ: Who cares any more about the final
grace-notes of a form of words – in the end. If not *for* you,
no, certainly not, but on your account, that's undeniable,
I became a murderer…now have to see, though,
it wasn't even necessary, the murder,
because you never knew, that I love you…
Of course you know, I cannot have had
another motive. You may even know
or think it possible, that I am not exactly from birth,
by nature, or from –
temperament, any kind of poisoner…so

if you at any rate grant me that:
what other than madness, for his having taken
you – Lena, you! away from me, what was it then?
What else could have made me into a murderer?

MAGDALENA: (*Desperate, shrugging but not indifferently.*)
Vanity? Revenge? Love, at any rate, which justified
the killing of someone for having destroyed it, love –
there cannot be such a love as that!
for people often love…

FRANZ: He destroyed it for us.

MAGDALENA: He did not, I did.
You killed the wrong one, the innocent.
Yes, unless you are going to –

FRANZ: I shall have to. And myself. The two of us.
I can feel now, how true it is what they say…
Since his death I think about it all the time:
that a murder changes the murderer.
weakens him totally. I don't even know
whether I can…
our little…our short night music, if I shall be able to
finish it…
The two of us both guilty
of his now being under the earth,
you the passive, I the active cause,
the two of us cannot possibly go on living
after this display of malice, not continue to stand each other
one day even, one night…

*He laughs basely.*

Absurd – fucking going on somewhere, with somebody,
possibly you with me even…and him, under the earth!
Won't do, never does: going on living. Not you. Not me.
Should have done it right away, straight,
before you'd got your shoes off back from his burial.
When you admitted, here, just now,

how you'd done it every day, a 'ritual'…
that's when I should have cut your throat, and then
                                                     mine after.
I only gave him poison a few times, in his drink
you gave him your cunt six times a week for years.
Which of us is the more hard-boiled?
'Are you still a virgin?'

*As he quotes this yet again, we can see how this overheard
intimacy has rendered him quite broken with jealousy; she is
now totally unpardonable.*

MAGDALENA: (*Who now understands how this has churned
him up; her tone is as wretched as nearly all defences in love
must be.*) I would never have told you, Franz.
You eavesdropped on us.

FRANZ: I know – your most intimate things were more
                                                        intimate,
so intimate, that not even now when it's all come out,
you can't even now bring the words out.

MAGDALENA: (*In pity now for his madness.*)
Oh, Franz, No, you know that
you were always a good lover.
It is not true, what you say, or – I don't know –
what you are afraid of, that there was something between
                                                     him and me,
– sexually, something particular! No Franz,
the most intimate things are the commonest. There is
                                                  nothing particular,
although probably all of us imagine there is.
If human beings ever show themselves as *not* being different
from each other, then it's in bed – that is the commonest!
How green must two people be, who give themselves airs
of doing better than others, what everybody does.

FRANZ: (*Bleakly.*)
Then why did you leave me to go to – him?

MAGDALENA: (*Now touches him again for the first time; she would like, though it is as desperate as it is useless, to bridge the gap that divides them for ever.*)
But Franz – he was alone!
Constanze had left him!
Her last child was by somebody else.
Because of his travelling, it cannot have been his,
As he – how often – told me.

FRANZ: As often as he came to you in the afternoons
For your 'lessons'…the reason
why Louise was given her notice so soon.

*He imitates her tone of voice, rather well.*

A servant-girl has nothing to do here, for me, just sits around,
a girl to run the errands is quite enough.
I should have had my ears examined at that…
I do not have a single colleague at the courts,
whose wife does not have a servant girl!
here in the Gruenangergasse there isn't a family
without one!

MAGDALENA: That's not true! The Melchiors and the
                                                                    Brinotskys
both have girls who come by the hour.

FRANZ: In the end music kept you so so busy,
that you neglected husband and daughter…
As if you women were ever worried
about whether your servants just sat around or worked.
You just have to have one as symbol of your position…
because you are always pleased that your husband
should have the highest possible expenses on your account…
the same as we men are so stupid
as to take coachman, not because we need one,
but because our position demands it of us.
Coachmen sit around not working even longer than
                                                                    servant girls.

MAGDALENA: You don't have a coachman –
Why should I need a girl!

FRANZ: Never mind that, everyone has servant girls but you;
but most of my colleagues do not have coachmen,
because having their own coach is far too dear.
A girl costs nothing, not really – everyone in our circles
has one.
How stupid, how contemptibly stupid of me,
first, not have noticed anything, secondly,
after I'd caught you at it, to forgive you,
in the crazy hope you'd accept the situation and stop.
Lena, have you for five minutes imagined
what it is like to look at oneself in the mirror
when you know, what I have known for all these years:
everyone knows, are you the only fool of the family,
your wife's tame idiot? I am the living proof
of the smoking-room riddle, if riddle it is:
'What does your wife's arsehole do
when she has an orgasm?'
Answer: 'He stays home and looks after the kids!'
But with us it wasn't even that –
at home was where you did it with him…
when he came to give his lessons!…

MAGDALENA: How do you know I didn't go to him?
Or maybe we met somewhere else?
He's got two summerhouses in the garden,
and after all his wife was in Baden the whole time!!

FRANZ: And how often did you have to farm Theresa out
somewhere?
Music wouldn't have bothered the child,
she was used to it dinning into her every day from us.

MAGDALENA: (*A miserable interjection, she is guilty.*)
She was not farmed out all the time.

FRANZ: (*With another push to the shoulder that almost knocks
her over.*) Oh – no? you mean you just got on with things
in front of her?

MAGDALENA: I told you, you are insane!

FRANZ: (*Prosaically.*) Well, why not?
A normal man, and even you will admit I'm that…
A harmless family man is betrayed by his wife,
though she must now and then have remembered she was
married to *him,*
betrayed him with his friend!

MAGDALENA: (*Decisive.*) You were never friends!

FRANZ: Oh, now and again, I think I can claim, maybe more:
that he had some respect for me as an amateur,
– and who wasn't an amateur beside him? –
how I played my instrument, in my modest way, but…

MAGDALENA: (*Disconsolate, as if she really had just grasped
how deeply her love affair had hurt him.*)
That is true, Franz, he would not, God knows,
have made music with just anyone but friends…

FRANZ: Call it what you like, it's true,
that he despised me as much as a man,
whose wife he had been dragging through the sheets
year after year, as he did as a weekend musician.

MAGDALENA: (*Louder again, passionately and with absolute
conviction.*) That is not true, Franz, that he ever –
not for one minute – despised you as a man. Never. Never!
You know – he was never a cynic.
On the contrary – how often did he say;
it is only because we are not taking
anything away from your husband, who still
has you and has no idea,
only because we do not want to hurt him,
can we go on with this!
I've told you that before.

FRANZ: (*Disbelieving.*)
'Not want to hurt him'!

MAGDALENA: Since you cannot – and I understand this –
                                                believe
    another word I say – here is one fact
    which you cannot get away from: Fondness, indeed,
    sympathy for you was what persuaded me to stay with you.
    After all, however much you despise me as a pianist,
    I make enough teaching, and at the Opera,
    to be able to live without you! So why, then,
    if not from fondness, should I have stayed with you?

FRANZ: (*With a shrug.*)
    Fear, motive enough! The courts would never
    have given you Theresa, if you had walked out on me,
    for a lover. There was enough talk about the two of you.
    If you had left me, it would have been *publishing* the truth!

MAGDALENA: And you could not, because of the child,
                                                Franz,
    Leave me with things unclear, as I did you…

FRANZ: You me? – to begin with,
    But since I have always known,
    You were still doing it…several times a week.

MAGDALENA: And you really cannot see any difference
    between sleeping with someone and killing them?

FRANZ: No, none! None at all!
    How often have the two of you murdered me,
    every time I thought, you were doing it again. I had no one.
    Adultery is the only crime,
    that can be forgiven solely by those who are also guilty of it.

MAGDALENA: That's why we must leave each other…
    not just separate, I mean out of the world!
    Everything could have been set to rights; not this:
    that you poisoned him, and worse,
    that you told me you had done so…almost with triumph.

FRANZ: If I had kept silent, it would have been no vengeance.
    How often has he triumphed over me, when he

as my wife so charmingly informed me –
could take you with his mouth, since you,
thanks to my abstinence, were once again a virgin…

*His face is so distorted, one can see he will never be able to
stand this. His look is now threatening, as it was at the
beginning of the scene, when she came home. There is a pause,
then…*

How you could have dared, since you knew
the girl was not here, and we should not be disturbed –
how dared you come home?
To be alone with me, in our four walls, I nearly said.
But they were, and they aren't any more
not for a long time, yours and mine, and now
yours and *his* four walls. Where,
if not where he fucks, is a man to be at home?
Perhaps in my, our sheets into the bargain?

*As he gets further into these measurelessly humiliating images
and pictures, one can see he is in the process of losing his
reason and again becoming a murderer.*

MAGDALENA: Have you gone crazy, you look like, no,
really.
I only came home again, because –
I'll leave tonight, get away from you tonight!

FRANZ: (*Laughs.*) You think you're getting out of here alive?
Leave me sitting here, for all Vienna to laugh at?

MAGDALENA: As if you still wanted to live with me,
*Could* still live with me!
Franz, let me do it myself.
It's better for the child, the lesser evil,
to have to tell herself, I am the daughter of a suicide,
rather than the daughter of a wife-murderer.
Let me have it in writing, now, at once,
my last wish from you,
that you take Theresa to my sister…

FRANZ: You are asking something from me? Ridiculous.

MAGDALENA: What is ridiculous is everything that
    brings about the end of our lives
    has brought about…but, please, my last request, Seriously.

FRANZ: (*With an idiotic laugh.*) 'Seriously' – you?

MAGDALENA: (*Goes to a little table, where there is paper,
    pen and ink, writes.*)
    Sign this, that you undertake, if I
    should die before you, to give our daughter to my sister…

FRANZ: (*As if actually considering the suggestion.*)
    What would persuade a married couple
    to sign such an insane document? Why? Have you
    ever heard of a husband, losing his wife, the mother
    of his only child, and then,
    unless he is cracked or perverted,
    giving away the woman's child? Why should he do that?

MAGDALENA: You just told me. Because he is cracked or
                                        perverted!
    You are both crazy and a murderer, if that's not grounds
                                        enough
    to bring my child at least out of reach of…a father like
                                        that?
    who says he will also become a wife-murderer, yes!
    I will spare you that, Franz,
    spare you, and more so, spare our child,
    from the need for you to do that.
    Let me do it myself.

FRANZ: (*As contemptuously as it is possible to say it.*)
    You'd never do it! Who's to guarantee
    that you'd *ever* keep your word and voluntarily atone
    for having made me the killer of your lover!

MAGDALENA: Why did you tell me about it –
    boast to me even?

FRANZ: (*Simply and honestly.*)
　　You don't listen – for revenge. Not mine on him
　　– to revenge myself on you, my confession was the only way.
　　You I loved – he was nothing to me...
　　You should have to go around for the rest,
　　however short, the rest of your days in the knowledge
　　of having him on your conscience. Should you have one!

MAGDALENA: (*Impressed by this cynical confession, and at
　　pains to match its tone in her answer.*)
　　Didn't even hate – but poisoned him.
　　And that took its time, not once and for all,
　　you repeated all the time,
　　every time you gave him Aqua Toffana in his drink...

FRANZ: It's not necessary all that often.

MAGDALENA: And he was – how did you put it? –
　　　　　　　　　　　　　　　　　　nothing to you.
　　So, just the means of putting the load onto me.
　　I would be guilty of the murder of my lover!

FRANZ: That is just how it was, yes.

MAGDALENA: How horrible you are, Franz, how revolting.
　　There was not even hate in you, when you –
　　and you always knew it! –
　　slowly poisoned the greatest musician of all time...
　　and not just the once, spontaneously...
　　no, but gradually you committed the murder
　　and for – *nothing.*
　　Everyone knows that poison doesn't work in single doses.

FRANZ: *Nothing?*

MAGDALENA: Nothing that could have meant anything to
　　　　　　　　　　　　　　　　　　　　　　you.

FRANZ: I had hate. Oh, yes, hate.
　　But not for him, of course,
　　for you: he could do nothing about it...even I

would not have been able to get away from you,
married to someone else, and seduced by you!
You are an image of lust, for which there is no antidote!
No antidote – just death.

MAGDALENA: (*After a slight pause.*)
How happily I would go to the scaffold
for having murdered you. But where to get a pistol?
You wouldn't even accept a bowl of soup from me now…
But now, after this last which you have loaded me with,
that you never even meant the murder for his sake,
but for me, then you can go for the rest of your days
with the deepest humiliation that can be
given to you: I am five months gone!
And *he* will live on in this child too.
Now I'll go and fetch Theresa, and tomorrow
at half-past five by the early coach,
I'll go to Bruenn, to my father.
Not *one* night, not ten minutes more will I stay with you.
My sister –

FRANZ: – will see nothing but your corpse!

*He gives a laugh, such as only comes from the pains of Hell,
picks up the razor which she flung away earlier, and attacks
her, as she begins to pull on her heavy overshoes, which she
took off at the start of the scene. He pushes her to the floor, in
order to slit her throat, and shouts out above her.*

A child of his – you will not bring into the world!
Live happily, when I am buried, sewn up in a cow-skin
for being a suicide – you really thought that?

*During these words, in part laboriously, hesitantly, in part
violently yelled out, they roll on the floor – a violent set-to.
Mortal terror gives the wife superhuman strength, to her voice
as well, as she tries to shake the furious man off her. He tears
her dress open at the neck, as if he wanted to slit her throat,
which he fails to do, as she manages several times to get on top
of him. She screams, as only those do in the grip of a knife-
wielding murderer, or of a fire.*

MAGDALENA: Help! Neighbours, help me,
Franz has gone mad, help, neighbours, come here, help.
Leave Theresa outside, but help me, Franz is killing me.
Break in the door – come, oh, hurry now.
Quickly. Help! Help me – help!

*Her cries are to be repeated as necessary, FRANZ also shouting.*

FRANZ: You won't be living any more
to bring a child into the world for him,
and I thrown out in the cow-skin of a suicide.

*It takes a long time, before she becomes unconscious, either
from her injuries or from fear. MAGDALENA has heard the
voice of the rescuer, also the yelling of her daughter, which
prompted the line to leave Theresa outside. We hear the loud
noise of the apartment door being broken in, not quickly, and
finally, since there is no other way, broken down. The mad
screaming of the child stops, clearly some neighbour has pulled
her into the next-door apartment to safety from the sight of
her parents' struggle. Then we hear the powerful voice of a
neighbour, calling loudly, desperately. He is in no way ignorant
of what is going on with the couple, since Mozart's visits to
MAGDALENA have naturally been known to the whole
house.*

NEIGHBOUR: (*Voice off. Repeating the words in different
orders.*) Franz, – don't be crazy! Let her go, Franz!
Have you gone mad?… Franz…let Lena live! Franz!

*This at the same time as MAGDALENA's fear-heightened
screams. Finally, after the struggle has lasted some while, she
is still; she no longer flails with her arms, nor with her feet.
As FRANZ stands up, thinking the unconscious woman is
dead, his clothing is seen to be wildly ripped and disordered;
he is bleeding profusely from his face and both hands. He
rises laboriously, his last strength having been needed to control
the panic-stricken woman with the razor, slashing her severely
in the neck, breast and one of her wrists. It is understandable
that he thinks her dead. For the rest of her life she will have*

*to wear shawls and scarves to cover the appallingly barbarous scars. He stares at her for a moment, at first in front of her on his knees, then standing up again – now he runs off into the darkened room next door, the couple's bedroom, since the apartment door has given under the strength of the axe-blows. We hear glass breaking and wood splintering. After this there is room for a man to enter. As he enters, we see him delay at MAGDALENA's body; he too takes her for dead, horrified he makes the sign of the cross, then turns and goes off into the dark room next door. His face has not been recognised; he will play the Emperor Joseph in the next scene.*

'Frau Hofdemel, who was so grievously mistreated by her husband, in a sudden access of maddened rage, is now, thanks to the skill and unremitting dedication of her doctors, Peter Rossmann and Guenther, sufficiently recovered to be able to express her thanks personally to certain highly and most-highly placed persons. How much the fate of this unfortunate woman has aroused the pity of almost every inhabitant of Vienna, how much everybody felt for her sufferings, is too well-known for us to have to make any reference to them here. Our great Empress has been kept informed of the lady's condition, given her comfort, and alleviated her suffering by the promise of future care for her. Many distinguished philanthropic friends have competed in comforting the unhappy woman and mitigating her sufferings. Particularly noticeable among these have been the Countess Starhremberg and the Countess Chotek...'

Graetzer Zeitung – 9th February 1792

Because of the excitement that the suicide of Hofdemel, and even more so the so nearly 'successful' attempt on his wife's life, had aroused in the whole huge monarchy – everyone spoke with horror of the two events – the Imperial family had also, demonstrably, to concern themselves with the recovery of Magdalena Hofdemel. The empress kept herself informed about the state of Magdalena's health, so that we may suppose Magdalena had, at first in a letter, since she was in hospital, and would hardly have been able to speak with her injuries, personally lobbied the Emperor to authorise the burial of her husband, instead of his being sewn up in a cow's hide and disposed of, the usual fate of suicides. This could be ordered by the Church or the Emperor only. Without doubt Magdalena was then received in private audience, just as Leopold, it is known, received the widow Constanze, in order to hear her request to be allowed to discharge Mozart's – albeit modest – debts with a performance of the Requiem, his final work. Constanze was certainly no more highly respected in Vienna than Magdalena, or she would have ventured to go, first to the thanksgiving in the church, secondly to the graveside, as her sister and Magdalena naturally did, along with one other woman.

The son of Maria Teresia, in his middle forties, had only become Emperor in the preceding year, on the early death of his brother, Joseph II – Leopold is also to die early, in the following year. Leopold, though less important, because less interested in reform than his brother, lives in some way with the art of his time, as the monarchs of the eighteenth century often did. This is in democracies entirely incomprehensible, with the single, brilliant exception of Pericles: de Gaulle took Malraux, France's most important author after Sartre, into the cabinet as Minister of Culture, Mitterand paid visits to Picasso and Juenger, but the interest that crowned heads so often used to display in artists and their work, does not occur in democracies. This is not only because artists, and those who are interested in them, are too inconsiderable as electoral potential, but also because, when democrats become politicians, they interest themselves only in interpreters, not originators, and then only when they have official jobs, like theatre intendants, or academy directors, but not in writers or composers.

Under princes, things were quite different; first, because the originators were as a rule the directors of the various institutes, that is, playwrights were the intendants, and composers the opera directors; secondly, and this above all, because the crowned heads were committed to art. The Emperor Joseph personally cut *The Marriage of Figaro*, albeit only the opera; the play, whose socially explosive content is not obscured by singing, was not performed at all; it remains the play which received the highest possible recognition from a figure in power, when Napoleon remarked of it: the French Revolution sprang from *The Marriage of Figaro*.

Emperor Leopold was therefore naturally cognisant of the fact that the successor of Frederick the Great had done his best to entice Mozart from Vienna to Potsdam, so as to be able to play music with him in the evenings. This King of Prussia, who, in 1787, immediately after his coronation, summoned Boccherini to Berlin as Court Composer, like his uncle played every evening, also composed. It was the age, in which, as far as the intimacy of artists and men in power is concerned, we find described in a letter of Lichtenberg, of 26 March 1781: 'A week ago today, the Duke of Weimar was here incognito, and, after visiting several professors, myself included, he rode to Magistrate Buerger, stayed some time with him, then commanded him to accompany him to Heiligenstadt, where he spent the night with him. Since that time people are saying that B. will also be going to Weimar, to swell the numbers of the saints already there. I don't believe it, although I would wish the good man might find repose in a cultivated court, he is not cut out for an official.'

This Duke of Weimar came on horseback, probably to persuade Lichtenberg and Gottfried August Buerger to his court, where he already enticed Goethe and Schiller. But Lichtenberg was a Professor of Physics, and Weimar was not a university town.

And the mother of this duke had brought Wieland and Herder to Weimar; and her mother – the sister of Frederick the Great, who had known Voltaire well – had brought Lessing to Wolfenbuettel; the Lessing who once wrote that every time he met the Duchess, she begged 'for another new play'. And finally the last descendant of these crowned heads, Wilhelm the Last of Germany, often visited, and also ennobled Menzel, gave the poet Liliencron a life pension, and as matter of course, would have spoken with his opera director, Richard Strauss, in the event of their meeting on Unter den Linden. For in those days, princes and chancellors, in contrast with today's democrats, went among their subjects without bodyguards, although the grandfather of that much-ridiculed Wilhelm the Last had twice been the object of pistol attempts on his life, as had Bismarck in Berlin. The Emperor Joseph, who had already made music with Mozart, spoke as a matter of course to him about his love for Constanze, known all over town, and of his coming marriage (16.1.82). On the 4.8.82, shortly after the marriage in St. Stephan's Cathedral, the Emperor, driving past the Mozarts in the Augarten, called out 'Three weeks married and quarrelling already?' Out walking, wanting to see how their dog would react, Mozart had pretended to strike his wife. It meant a great deal to Mozart that the Emperor attended his concerts: 'his satisfaction was measureless, – he sent 25 ducats.' The intimacy of courts and 'their' artists has never appeared in democratic times...for which, naturally, the lack of relationship between the public and works of art is partly to blame: it says in 'Faust' 'What you call the spirit of the age – that is the spirit of your masters.' Where, however, the masters have no visible relationship to art, then their subjects, we democrats, will also not deem it necessary to bother about such a relationship... Thus today's masters know – and knowledge means interest – almost nothing about the artists of their time. If dictatorship is the tyranny of the uniformed, then democracy is the tyranny of the uninformed. The cultivated Emperor Leopold is quite aware that he and his empire have Magdalena Hofdemel alone to thank for Mozart's not having left Vienna for London or Berlin. For the fact that Mozart's marriage was played out, had been made known to the public, in the hair-raisingly honest unconventional manner of the time, by Constanze's moving away from her husband, to Baden, the only possible reason for her not appearing at his funeral, which, in itself, was so chillingly honest, that, two hundred years on, we still get excited about it.

We should not forget that, at this time, the ducal residence city of Weimar, Goethe's Weimar, had only six thousand inhabitants; of course Vienna was twenty times the size, but still, by present-day standards hardly to be thought of as a world centre: in that gossip-ridden nest everyone knew everything – if not about everybody, then certainly about everybody famous. Mozart's death had not yet been announced in the press – certainly, on orders from higher up, not to be so before the funeral – before crowds of sympathisers had gathered in front of the house.

# Scene 2 – Epilogue

*A circular room built and decorated in the wonderful early baroque style of the Vianna Hofburg, showing no similarity with the bourgeois-modern, that is classical Empire music room of the Hofdemels, built three generations after this room. In the fireplace, which is almost too big for the room, a fire has been lit.*

*The FOOTMAN, in pale blue livery, with white wig and white stockings to his lilac breeches and buckled shoes, who now shows MAGDALENA into the so-called 'small' music room that Leopold sometimes uses for audiences, is no more than the personification of a bow. He certainly lets it be seen that he is not introducing a 'person of consequence', but a mere civilian, and, in his eyes – and anyone who is only a footman has a more highly-developed sense of 'consequence' than the ordinary person – her only merit lies in the fact that His Majesty has granted her a private audience.*

*The FOOTMAN has opened the double doors, stage left, so that his face is not seen, as he is the same actor as played FRANZ. Nor should his voice be recognisable; he merely says, after MAGDALENA has walked past him into the room, and he is shutting the doors behind them both:*

FOOTMAN:…and if you please,
His Majesty expressly requested
you pass the time as you desire at one of the instruments,
until such time as he can grace you with his presence.
The newest music can be found – there!

> *He gestures once again, with a half-bow, towards the music lying on a small, rococo table by the spinet, and goes out.*

MAGDALENA: (*While he shuts the single wing of the double door which he had opened.*)
Thank you, but I have Mozart's last pages with me.

> *MAGDALENA today, is wearing a black two-pointed hat, not the three-pointed one of the first scene, and, until the Emperor comes in, she is veiled. She has taken off her cloak outside, and is wearing elegant, but utterly undecorated*

*widow's weeds, and carries a black bag, since, in these days of mourning and shock, she needs quite a number of handkerchiefs. The 'Requiem' manuscript is contained in a pearl-sewn, colourful case, a large so-called Pompadour, with a silver clasp and chain. In consequence of the January cold after the snow, she is again wearing her sturdy street shoes. She removes one of her gloves, lifts the veil away from her eyes, and immediately becomes immersed in a book of music, clearly newly-printed which she has eagerly picked off the spinet, her curiosity aroused. She can be seen to be reading the notes, as a practising musician, so to speak with her whole body. As she reads, she is almost playing, but soon lays the music aside and sits at the spinet and plays, by heart, the opening of the 'Requiem'...*

*But what is mainly noticeable are the traces of her wounds; the razor slashes were so severe that for the rest of her life, she will be forced to wear scarves, and shawls to hide them. Years later, after she had trusted herself to come back to Vienna, which she had left immediately after her husband's funeral, to seek refuge with her father in Bruenn, and to bring her and Mozart's child into the world. Carl Czerny reported that even at this time she was still wearing shawls, so that her fearfully scarred neck and shoulders – and by the end of the Eighteenth century the shoulders were often exposed – should not be seen. Beethoven put off MAGDALENA's request to be allowed to visit him repeatedly, saying: 'Hofdemel? No, that is the woman who had that business with Mozart.' As uptight an upright citizen as he was great as an artist, – who probably, like Menzel, lived all his life without a woman – he repeatedly refused her admittance. When, finally, he played for her, she, as a pianist, pronounced: 'Even better than Mozart in improvisation.'*

*Now the two wings of the double doors are opened – from outside into the circular room, and equally violently shut behind His Majesty, the footman being this time unseen, and the Emperor LEOPOLD enters quickly, Magdalena having immediately stopped playing. Five steps away from the forty-*

*three-year-old, who still sports a pigtail and short powdered wig, she sweeps a highly accomplished court curtsey, her forehead nearly touching the floor. The Emperor, charming, a son of the Rococo, as 'free-thinking' as a second son of Maria Teresia, as his predecessor and, as a reformer, much-envied brother, steps forward with more friendliness than politeness and almost picks her up from the floor.*

*She speaks in no more than a breath.*

Your Majesty had the goodness to…

LEOPOLD: No, no, you must not stop playing…it is twice now
that I have heard you;
at the Schwarzenbergs and at Count Thun's.

MAGDALENA: Yes, Majesty, the two high points of my life,
Your Majesty's presence!

LEOPOLD: (*Laughing then speaking with an actorish intimacy.*)
That is something we would not wish for you,
my dear Frau Hofdemel,
that the mere presence of a man, while you were playing,
could be a high point of your life.
Certainly you should not be saying so now,
now that he is dead, poor Mozart:
to have been his friend, Mozart's friend, *that* would
without any doubt, have been the highest
that life could have offered you!

MAGDALENA: The highest, yes,
and the most painful too, Majesty.
it was only the fact that I…would have killed
his child inside me, prevented me
from following him in death!
That is why I – I can at this moment think of nothing
other than those talks with him –
why I just now was playing a few bars
of his 'Requiem'. How kind of Your Majesty,
to grant permission through your servant,
for me to make use of Your Majesty's instrument.

LEOPOLD: (*Excited by this information as only an impassioned music-lover could be; Mozart's legacy interests him more than anything. He has failed to catch the fact that she was pregnant by Mozart, particularly as she has come on account of her husband – nearly all requests for an audience had to be accompanied by the reason for it.*)
You know – but of course – his last work!
Tell us, please, something,
no, *play* us something from the 'Requiem'!

MAGDALENA: (*Sketches a curtsey.*)
If Your Majesty would have the goodness to accept
the 'Requiem', – though unfinished –
I have permitted myself to have a copy of the manuscript
made for Your Majesty, and would beg Your Majesty
to pass the message to Her Majesty the Empress
Her Majesty, in her infinite goodness, had my doctors,
Rossmann and Guenther, inform her about my condition
on two occasions –
that in the next few days I shall have had
a copy of the keyboard concerto prepared
that Mozart composed for me.

LEOPOLD: How thoughtful of you to have gone to the trouble
of having had a copy prepared for us!

MAGDALENA: It was no trouble, Majesty – what am I
to busy myself with now, if not with Mozart!

LEOPOLD: (*Leafing through the manuscript, handed to him with a court curtsey.*)
How kind, you really have our gratitude, Frau Hofdemel!
Frau Mozart was here yesterday, asking us to allow her
quite understandably – the first performance of the Requiem
in consideration of his actually quite minimal debts.

MAGDALENA: (*And we can recognise her hate of Constanze.*)
Debts? – it would be new to me, Your Majesty,
to hear that Mozart had any debts.
If Majesty will permit, I would interpret that

statement from his…his widow somewhat like the fact
that she did not make an appearance at the funeral.
What does Frau Constanze,
who after all lives in Baden, which certainly
made expenses for him, know about his end?

LEOPOLD: (*Somewhat disdainfully: he knows how women
speaking of rivals, actual or imagined, always make themselves
as ridiculous as men do when talking about professional
colleagues, whether competitors or not.*)
Well, let us leave that, Frau Mozart has her bereavement
as you, my dear, have yours.
You, Frau Hofdemel, have two of them!
All Vienna is in an uproar – much much more,
because your husband wanted to murder you, and had
therefore to kill himself, poor fellow,
than because of Mozart's death,
which for those of us close to him cannot be said
to have come as a total surprise.
Let us sit down, as you have a great deal to tell me.
What does an Emperor ever find out at first hand?

*LEOPOLD indicates a pair of early baroque armchairs, about
a hundred years old, that is from around 1650. She waits,
naturally, until he is sitting, than, with a quick bob, she sits
herself. There is no table between the two matching chairs,
this fashion only having come in once sofas and chairs ceased
to be placed against the walls. Here the monarch and his
visitor are at least six metres apart – just as de Gaulle would
later place his visitors…*

MAGDALENA: Your Majesty will surely have the goodness
to understand I am unable to find sufficient peace of mind
to talk of Mozart, before Your Majesty has had the goodness
to allow my most humble entreaty
to forbid the cruel priests of St. Stephan's
to take my husband, whose mind was disturbed –
how can it have been any otherwise? –
and in unchristian fashion, as a suicide
throw him out onto the knacker's rubbish-heap…

LEOPOLD: (*With cautious but understandable scepticism.*)
    Frau Hofdemel, your husband was known to us
    and esteemed by us, as one of the cleverest, the most
                                  circumspect
    of lawyers and officers in the Imperial service…
    This makes it truly difficult
    to declare him as having been of unsound mind…

MAGDALENA: (*With almost infectious passion, which will
    finally induce a change of mind in the Emperor.*)
    But then Your Majesty must *know* the poor man
    could only have committed the attempted murder
    and the murder of himself in complete confusion of mind!
    The church cannot make Hofdemel
    mentally responsible for the godless suicide!
    Someone so *circumspect*, as Your Majesty
    had the infinite goodness to describe Hofdemel,
    *cannot* have been in his right mind
    when he committed the mortal sin of self-slaughter…
    Majesty, please – Your Majesty please to look at me,
    the scarves, the bandages.
    Your Majesty's first physicians in Vienna,
    did not want to let me leave the hospital.
    I was only able to, because I had to say quickly to Your
                                Majesty,
    the priests will throw my husband into the suicides' corner,
    unless Your Majesty intervenes at once…
    Both doctors are ready to bear witness,
    they have assured me, that my unhappy husband
    must have lost his reason, when he tried
    to cut my throat, as he then did his own!
    The mere fact he did not succeed with me, so the doctors
                                    say,
    since it is so easy, just *one* determined cut,
    if performed with true premeditation, proves
    Hofdemel was entirely devoid of understanding.

LEOPOLD: (*Coolly – he recognises she is not telling the truth.*)
    Reason enough remaining, to kill himself afterwards

to escape being broken on the wheel,
and then beheaded. We have every sympathy for the
unhappy man...
Nothing that we hear from you here, please be assured,
Frau Hofdemel,
will leave these four walls –
but if you could explain, at least to *Us,*
something I find quite inexplicable:
that such a reliable, discreet officer of justice,
such a...quite incredible, dear lady,
that he should have lost his reason!
Quite unbelievable, yes. I mean, unless you can give
a reason to Us – in confidence, of course.

MAGDALENA: Reason? –
*Can* there be any sort of reason,
where Reason itself has gone?
Look at me, Majesty! A dreadful sight, is it not?
The doctors tell me, as long as I live,
I shall never be able to go into the streets
without a shawl, the scars are there for ever.
As Your Majesty was good enough to say
how he had valued my husband
what can have happened to him
other than total insanity, for him to believe
that he had to murder me!
And then himself,
to cut his own throat!

LEOPOLD: (*Slightly irritated, impatient.*)
Yes, yes, you have said so more than once.
But why, my dear – *why* did your husband
so suddenly and completely lose his reason?
Is it true that it happened after coming back from the
funeral?

MAGDALENA: Yes, an hour after,
a painful hour, filled with, I must admit,
all too justified reproaches.

I was astonished, indeed appalled, to find
my husband at home and not in his office.
And I blamed him, drastically,
for his not, as he should have done,
as a friend, as a lodge brother,
Hofdemel had three weeks before this
been received as a mason,
because Mozart had opened up the way for him...

LEOPOLD: We know about it. We are also a mason...

MAGDALENA: (*With a nod.*)
Because he had not been at the burial,
not even in the chapel either, I blamed Hofdemel.
Because I had absolutely relied on that, that's why
I had given our child to the neighbours, I was so sure
that Hofdemel would come after work, straight to the burial.
But since I found him, to my anger, at home,
playing music at that,
I blamed him, and violently, for not paying the last honours
to a friend, a genius!
Not even because of claims of work,
but from spite. Sitting at home, playing music,
while under the earth, Mozart...

*Unable to continue, she weeps soundlessly, taking a
handkerchief from the black, pearl-embroidered handbag.*

LEOPOLD: A quarrel, and a justified one, I can understand,
but a quarrel is one thing, my dear Hofdemel,
killing your wife – quite another!
So, let me have the truth, please – or I cannot,
*will* not tell lies for your poor husband.
I cannot tell Blessed and Merciful Holy Mother Church,
as she still calls herself, it was mental illness
drove Hofdemel to suicide!

MAGDALENA: (*Now sobbing.*)
The cow-hide is already there –
Those barbarians at St Stephan's,

as Sophie, Constanze's sister, calls them,
because they refused to send a priest,
as long as Mozart was still alive…

LEOPOLD: (*Furious.*)
What! A priest, only after he was dead! We didn't know that.
That is unchristian, unforgiveable!

MAGDALENA: (*Nods.*)
Yes, Majesty, the monsters went so far as to say
Mozart his whole life had been too bad a Catholic…

LEOPOLD: Of course all Vienna knew of his excesses,
but what we have just heard, that they sent no priest
as he lay dying, that they can never justify,
the gentlemen of St Stephan's!

MAGDALENA: (*Quickly talking over him, as if he had not said this.*) They've thrown the cow-hide in front of my door,
a neighbour told me, visiting me in hospital this morning,
the cow-hide I have to sew him into,
my poor husband – they don't allow him a burial
in Jesus. Barbarians…as if a man, father, official –
*madness,* he…

*LEOPOLD has risen violently, takes three steps, then speaks,
almost in an ultimatum, certainly and clearly meaning to
prevent Hofdemel's memory from being sullied by the church
which he – like his late brother Joseph in the highest degree –
loathes.*

LEOPOLD: Well, then – now, in honesty: *what* happened,
and *how?*
Hofdemel, or anyone else for that matter,
would not have brought the razor,
fetched it from the next room, to murder his wife,
because she was nagging him,
for not having attended the funeral of his friend,
a genius, as you say…
Never, since human beings have had to bury one another,

has that been grounds for murdering one's consort...never!
We are sorry that you not only tell lies to your Emperor,
but also to the man to whom you are appealing for help!
Now, for the last time or we shall have to terminate this...

*MAGDALENA who had also got up when he did, now sits*
*again, on a gesture from him. For all her accomplished twisting*
*and turning, she finally knows she can only hide one of the*
*two truths from a man as clever as LEOPOLD, namely that*
*Hofdemel had been the poisoner of Mozart, but not the second*
*truth, that Mozart had been the father of her child. This is*
*why she has already, and not without pride, stated the fact,*
*even if it had gone unremarked in the first moment,*
*LEOPOLD's interest in Mozart's last composition having*
*submerged it.*

MAGDALENA: Majesty, my most humble duty.
I beg you not to suppose that I would dare
to lie directly to Your Majesty.
But in matters of love no one can make a statement,
without always making the same statement for at least
one other person, mostly for two others...and how
when, as here, the two are dead,
is one to beg for permission
to speak with such unrestrained honesty
as if it were solely a matter of oneself!

LEOPOLD: (*Laughs, and speaks with great irony, not without*
*affection, but with sympathy for a clever woman.*)
Very clever, Madame, excellent the way
you establish your moral duty of silence!
However, we shall absolve you of it – just as cleverly –
just as we, as is well known, are by the Grace of God,
Supreme Head of the royal and imperial Austro-Hungarian
                                                    Empire,
so are we Supreme Head of the one True blessed and
                                                holy church
in these lands. You know this quite well, my dear Hofdemel,
or why else should you have come to us to demand an
                                                Act of Grace

from us to confer Christian burial upon a suicide –
something we have known from childhood up
was utterly unthinkable, unless your good departed –

*He crosses himself.*

and may peace be with him –
had not lost his reason, when he judged himself
after his murderous attack on you, his wife!
What you have said here, and we repeat ourselves,
is as secret, more secret than in any confessional.
now we must make a request: that you tell no one
that it was the Emperor, that we –
and your note from yesterday has therefore
been burnt with our own hand in a candle –
that is was we, who directed the Church
to bury Hofdemel in consecrated ground!

MAGDALENA: (*Spontaneously grasping his hand and kissing it.*)
Oh Majesty!
Your Majesty is so great. So good! Majesty, truly, Hofdemel
had lost his reason. How gravely, Majesty may judge
in that he left me for dead, in my own blood, unconscious;
that he was no longer even capable of finding
whether I was still breathing…
He had come at me with a scream
that it could not happen,
that I would be delivered of Mozart's child,
while he would have to kill himself.
He thought I was dead, Majesty, really,
when he struck himself down with one blow:
it is as the doctors said, Herr Rossman and Herr Guenther,
with an unheard of energy.
That it was very hard, they said, to cut one's own throat,
And so easy to cut someone else's.
That is what the doctors said,
no one could do it *unless* they were insane!

LEOPOLD: (*Making himself out denser than he is.*)
What did you say just then?

Delivered of *Mozart's* child?
Delivered? – but you are already a mother!

MAGDALENA: (*Curtseys, then, quietly not without the pride
which in women, if it is a matter of pregnancy, is stronger
than shame.*)
Yes, Your Majesty, and will continue so, if God has let
the child of my body survive Hofdemel's murderous attack.

LEOPOLD: But why – why in the name of God,
why did Hofdemel have to…no:
why did he *think* he had to *kill* himself?
For God's sake, a man so valued in the world
and at court too, what had he *done*,
to think he had to kill himself?

*MAGDALENA has said too much. More for the sake of
Hofdemel's child than for herself she had sworn to herself
never to betray that Hofdemel had poisoned Mozart, nor even
to express it as a suspicion. Thus she is now forced to invent
a reason.*

*That Hofdemel should have killed himself after his apparently
'successful' attempt on his wife's life, is plausible enough. He
would have been sentenced to death…but why should a hitherto
highly-placed jurist in a highly-regarded position, have
murdered his wife? She can only make the insane deed halfway
believable by confessing that she had brought her husband to
the edge of his reason by revealing that not he, but Mozart,
was the father of her unborn child.*

MAGDALENA: (*Inhibited, but not without a certain
accompanying pride.*)
I did it, Majesty, *I* drove him to madness –
I alone am responsible for his death…even for
his committing suicide. Although he
was a Freemason, he was always a churchgoer,
sceptical certainly, but a true believer, yes, Majesty,
he would never have done it.
It was *my* fault – alone, forgive ne, Majesty.

LEOPOLD: (*While she is silent, but for her tears.*)
    We have nothing to forgive here, nothing at all, that is
                                          something
    you must take up with God…but we would
    so like to *understand*. What can you have done
    to make your husband imagine he must kill himself?
    And in consequence, not allow you to live, even though with
    child, as we now hear. What had *you* done, *he* done?
    We ask this for the last time.
    If you refuse an explanation, then we
    shall not be able to grant the Act of Grace!
    The more you conceal, the more colourful it becomes…
    We begin, however improbable it seemed until yesterday,
    when the widow Mozart maintained
    that he had been quite convinced,
    since midsummer, that he was being poisoned.
    We begin to see our loyal Hofdemel as not unconnected
    with this conviction of Mozart's, who – God knows – we
    knew well enough not to have been able to find a trace
    of persecution mania, or a wish
    to make himself more interesting than he was.
    True – or do you not agree, Frau Hofdemel?

MAGDALENA: (*Now much on her guard; no one could
recognise the cunning with which she distracts from the theme
of poisoning. Anyone who suddenly admits and confesses the
second worst fact, distracts most effectively from the very worst.*)
    Majesty, no one who was close to Mozart
    had not heard from his own mouth, for months,
    that he was being poisoned.
    He stated so quite clearly more than once.

LEOPOLD: Possibly because it was – true! Baron Swieten,
    just like Mozart's widow, confirmed what you say.
    It is going a little far, explaining it away as imagination,
    when two doctors had seen *and said nothing*
    about the body being swollen up as in cases of poisoning!
    Why should Mozart have just imagined it?
    Because such an accusation was a terrible condemnation

of the world he lived in? Perhaps genius has its price
and one which corresponds to its greatness?
What would we know… I would not presume to doubt
anything that Mozart said as a certainty.

MAGDALENA: And for that very reason, Majesty…
Because he suspected, knew it –
as he shed tears saying farewell to Haydn, saying to him
he would not see him again…

LEOPOLD: Baron Swieten informed us
the two doctors had not reported the swelling of the body,
thinking it for the best, that Mozart should be buried,
not in the specially purchased grave, but in a common grave
with others, to make later examinations difficult…

*This is, in fact, the only possible explanation for Mozart's not
being buried in the grave Swieten had purchased for him.*

When two reputable doctors keep silent,
that silence is the most eloquent of proofs,
the proof *ex silentio.*

MAGDALENA: Forgive me, Majesty, I have no Latin –
*Ex silentio?*

LEOPOLD: A suppressed proof, that is,
One that one cannot adduce as evidence.

MAGDALENA: Thank you, Majesty!
But should not Your Majesty have ordered an autopsy,
if the doctors had found no explicable cause of the swelling?

LEOPOLD: Why? – if it was true!
That he had been poisoned, then why
dig the final confirmation from an autopsy?
His widow stated to us yesterday, that he
had said to her already in July:
'I know I am going to die: someone has given me
Aqua Toffana.' Was it your husband, Frau Hofdemel?
He was, after all, capable of a double murder!

And why else should someone kill himself,
instead of feeling relief at the death of a rival?

MAGDALENA: Because I was five months with child by
that rival.
That first, Majesty. And second:
because my husband had believed
he would have to kill me, had killed me.
Motive enough to kill himself, for a man, Majesty,
robbed of his reason by jealousy,
and still jealous of the dead man,
knowing his child lived on inside me!

LEOPOLD: Not bad, not bad at all,
the way you – not to burden your first child,
Hofdemel's child, with a father who murdered Mozart,
the way you digress from the unavoidable…
yes, quite unavoidable suspicion,
that your husband poisoned Mozart.
Which we also believe, now that you tell us
you were in your fifth month, by Mozart.
Your husband, Frau Hofdemel, this is what we suspect,
did *not* originally mean to kill you and then himself,
because you were with child by Mozart,
but because he learned, after Mozart was dead,
learned like the rest of Vienna, the corpse was so swollen,
the doctors said, only Aqua Toffana could have done it.
Which only confirms what Mozart
had suspected since the previous summer.
But if it could not have been anything but the poison,
causing the swelling, who could have had a motive
other than the man whose wife Mozart had taken,
and indeed made pregnant? Who else, Frau Hofdemel,
who else knows about Mozart's fatherhood?

MAGDALENA: (*With a reflex sketch of a curtsey.*)
No one, since my husband's death, Majesty, no one else,
other than your Majesty and myself.
Perhaps Mozart's widow – but she would suppress it,
indeed, she would vehemently deny it,

considering her own last child
was not Mozart's any more, but Suessmayr's!
But, Majesty, my husband – and I can prove it –
was innocent of poison, insofar as
there was any in Mozart's death,
since it was just five minutes before
Hofdemel tried to kill me, that he discovered
I was pregnant and Mozart was the father.

LEOPOLD: (*With a laugh.*)
Come now – no wife can be five months gone
without her husband noticing! Do you mean:
he knew I was pregnant – he just did not know
it was by Mozart! And how, if you will forgive me,
oo *you* know that with such certainty?

MAGDALENA: (*Hard.*)
A woman always knows that, Majesty.
We had not been together as man and wife for a long time.
We slept apart, Hofdemel could have failed to see that I…

LEOPOLD: Which only goes to indicate
how justifiably murderous poor Hofdemel was!
How could such an reasonable, clever man,
but *only* reasonable and clever, like Hofdemel,
how could he defend himself against a rival
as famous, and as a person,
anything like as attractive as your…our good Mozart?

MAGDALENA: Majesty – I implore you!

*And she has actually fallen to her knees; he raises her, warding
her off, painfully moved, and speaks angrily.*

LEOPOLD: Do not confuse us with an altar!
Stand up – or we shall put an end to this audience…

MAGDALENA: Forgiveness, Majesty, my desperate situation –
I do not wish to leave this room
without convincing Your Majesty
my husband may have been confused, insane – but no
murderer!

LEOPOLD: Not a murderer?
A wife-murderer, even with child...

MAGDALENA: Precisely because no one can demonstrate
it as convincingly
as Your Majesty has just done:
precisely because Hofdemel had a motive
with his friend – they were friends, Majesty,
often playing music, eating together...

LEOPOLD: A friend who after all stole his wife!

MAGDALENA: Yes, but precisely because Hofdemel
admittedly, I confess,
had a motive like no other man for miles around,
it cannot have been *him* that poisoned Mozart,
why else would I so frankly tell Your Majesty
that I was with child by Mozart?
Had I been able to cause the slightest suspicion, Majesty,
that Hofdemel had done it, had been capable of
murdering Mozart,
I would have kept silent, for my daughter's sake,
about the fact that I would give birth, in four month's time,
to a child of Mozart's.
No, Majesty, Hofdemel was incapable of committing a
murder!

LEOPOLD: (*Soberly.*) No body is incapable of murder...
Hofdemel, for example – his wife and himself.
It depends on the situation.
...how else would any man volunteer
to serve in an aggressive war??
Calm yourself,
we do not doubt, Frau Hofdemel,
that you are convinced of your husband's innocence!
But why do you demand that *we* should be equally
convinced?
Why not believe Mozart's doctors and von Swieten?
Why not just accept that his body
bore traces of poisoning?

Do not let yourself be drawn into any dispute.
What difference can it make to you, that your Emperor
should believe what everybody says,
that Mozart was poisoned –
what difference does it make, that we believe it?
We shall allow your petition,
in that we shall order the Church,
to give Hofdemel Christian burial…
We shall also prevent a post-mortem
which could possibly give information about a
                              perpetrator…
But with that, my dear, let there be an end to it. *Please!*

*This last word is final, imperative.*

We believe you to be convinced of your husband's
                              innocence.
We do not, however, believe anything else about it
and have no wish to discover anything
that could bring our residence so into discredit
that people would say if Mozart had followed
calls to become Court Composer in Berlin or London,
he would still be alive today!

MAGDALENA: Oh, Your Majesty has just touched on the
                              most unbearable,
and to me the most unforgiveable thing of all.
Mozart would still be alive, had he not lived with me.
It was for me, expressly for me,
he wrote his most moving Piano Concerto.

*Here one can only agree with Francis Carr, that the concertos
K.449, K.453, K.482 (dedicated to Babette Ployer), K.456
(to Maria Teresia von Paradis) and K.595 (most probably to
Magdalena Hofdemel) were of a quite different calibre from
those dedicated to Constanze. All three women were piano
pupils of Mozart and naturally the dedications were influenced
by this fact. No one should ignore the fact that a piano concerto
affords a composer the ideal opportunity for a portrait,*

*particularly if in performance the subject of the portrait is the soloist.*

LEOPOLD: You mean his last concerto?
Yes, indeed, most affecting.

MAGDALENA: Number twenty-seven.

LEOPOLD: Yes, we know it: B-flat.
But how difficult it is!
You will have to give us some lesson on it!

MAGDALENA: I would be so glad to be able to play it for
Your Majesty…
But, if possible, in the next few days,
if I may beg in all humility,
for I have to leave Vienna, at once;
I cannot run the gauntlet here,
where everyone knows everyone else's business.

LEOPOLD: (*Nods and smiles.*)
I mean it, you must play it for us…
If Mozart stayed in Vienna for your sake,
instead of obeying calls to Potsdam or to London,
and if poison is supposed to have killed him

*In the tone of an ultimatum; he wishes to make an end, the theory of Murder not fitting in with raison d'etat.*

as he himself thought, and which we
nevertheless do not even wish to know,
it is too far beyond the bounds of taste,
then Mozart's suspicion can only have been
in the direction of your husband!

MAGDALENA: (*Decisively, knowing now for certain that the Emperor speaks the truth.*)
Mozart would have told me, Majesty. No, Majesty, in that
case
he would have stopped keeping company with my husband.
But he did not.

LEOPOLD: (*Not to be confused by any of her convincingly
produced lies; he smiles now, one of the few people placed as
highly as he is, who nevertheless have deep knowledge of human
nature.*)
How could he have done, without putting both of you
in jeopardy. Even you know that!
We believe that you believe what you are saying.
But how are you to know, my dear Frau Hofdemel,
that it is your entirely normal and natural instincts
making you believe your husband cannot have given
the Aqua Toffana to Mozart? In point of fact –
and this is tormenting you – Hofdemel had endless
opportunity and was the only one with a motive!
Let us put it frankly: desire for vengeance.
Let us not judge him, your husband. He has atoned.
How desperate he must have been.
He loved you, Frau Hofdemel.

MAGDALENA: Your Majesty, can someone if he loves me,
murder my lover?

LEOPOLD: *Only* then.
And perhaps not only can, but must.
Since we view the Church and its teaching with some
scepticism,
let us take out directions in morality from the antique:
from that emperor who died here in Vienna,
sixteen hundred years ago, Marcus Aurelius.
He tells us, first, to 'leave men with their sins',
and secondly 'sentence more mildly than the law requires.'
We feel that emperor had us men in power directly in
mind…

We, at any rate, follow his maxims.
Even without that, we have little inclination
to challenge the 'barbarians of St Stephan'
as you, Frau Hofdemel, describe the clergy,
and rightly, since they were not even prepared
to send a priest to Mozart's death-bed.

Let us rather study rules of behaviour in literature –
the Germans have got a new poet, name of Goethe, a wild,
but – in our view – entirely honest,
perhaps for that reason, honest man.

MAGDALENA: My husband also read his 'Sorrows of
Young Werther', Majesty.
How often I had to think – how could I not think? –
of the last sentence in the book,
when poor Werther dies, like my Hofdemel,
by his own hand:
'No priest accompanied him.'

LEOPOLD: Isn't that so? A poet, compelling, because
merciful.
Shocking, but how honest though, when he also writes,
and we read it with horror, but understanding,
this Goethe writes, he could not imagine
any crime he himself could not commit…
It makes a man careful, anxious indeed,
who has the difficult office of passing judgment.
And that is why we shall demand of the Church,
that your husband, so much to be pitied,
shall be given a priest to his burial.
We say this to you, confident
that you will thank us by concealing it from the world.

MAGDALENA: (*Almost, but not quite, falling on her knees again.*)
Majesty – how could I abuse your Majesty's kindness
by speaking of it? By the light of my Theresa's eyes,
and of Mozart's child inside me –
I shall never breathe a word of Your Majesty's
proof of grace or of this audience.

*LEOPOLD's sympathy for her has increased, perhaps also
because of her beauty, which her mourning dress and her
weeping have done nothing to lessen, but if anything have
increased.*

LEOPOLD: We are not unmoved that a woman should with
such passion
entreat us for Christian burial for a husband,
who, after all, had tried to murder her...
Your humanity has reawakened our own!
We tell ourselves: judge not that ye be not judged!
Can we tell what *we* would have done,
with someone against whom we would have so little chance
as Everyman against Mozart, had he robbed us of our wife,
perhaps our lover even! And Hofdemel? A lawyer
against Mozart,
is pitting a hatter against the Good Lord!
How could your Hofdemel so much as bear
to look at himself in the mirror,
without perpetually thinking: I'll get even with him!

MAGDALENA: Majesty, I am shaken, because Majesty is so...
So right. I often used to say:
'Find somebody else, Franz!' –
I didn't betray him for long, not any more,
since he knew about us.
And then – we could still speak of it to each other,
civilised – he said, with regret, but truth;
if one is inclined to fidelity, one is also sentenced to it.
I cannot take another –
I love you, you...murderess!
Yes, Majesty, he called me – murderess!
As I now know – rightly!

LEOPOLD: (*Nodding.*)
Yes, because he already knew he would, he must –
become a murderer! Because of you. *Because of you,* Frau
Hofdemel.

When was this, then?

MAGDALENA: In the late summer.

LEOPOLD: Then Mozart was right, when he told his wife
first in June or July, I know someone has given me Aqua
Toffana!

73

MAGDALENA: But, Majesty, not Hofdemel!
It was when I came back from Mozart's burial,
he first heard that I was pregnant by him!

LEOPOLD: Now do not start all that over again,
after this Act of Grace it would be ungrateful…
You are doing it so we shall, for the sake of Hofdemel's child,
declare him innocent of the poisoning; but, you know,
he suffered like an animal, your husband,
because no one can bear to lose a woman like you in this
way,
without hitting back, in any way he can.
Well, Hofdemel could, he *could* kill him, kill his rival…
We would have done that, since we could, no more
than Hofdemel, be a rival of Mozart's.
To be a rival of someone –
as our good mother, God rest her soul, said of Mozart,
sent by God and blessed by God…

*He is forced to laugh.*

Prince Kaunitz, and God rest *his* soul too,
already said, often, to my late mother:
a city that has a Mozart
must never let him go, anywhere where he is tempted;
and he was away, yes, for a year at a time, twice,
in London or Paris! With such rarity it should not be
allowed.
Nor have we allowed it any further,
our brother and ourselves…and you still more,
Frau Hofdemel, did not allow it, Mozart's going
to Potsdam or London!
And now his staying here has been the death of him…
Ach, what are men, that they should make plans –
did he know that you were with his child…

MAGDALENA: (*Proudly.*)
However not? Naturally, of course, Your Majesty.
His last pleasure!

LEOPOLD: (*Benevolently, almost amused.*)
How does a husband know, Frau Hofdemel,
whether the children are his or a rival's?

MAGDALENA: (*Quite seriously.*)
Admittedly, Majesty, the men can never know that,
thanks be to God – but we women do!

*With unintentional pride.*

Since His Majesty the King of Prussia tried
to persuade Mozart – several times –
to come to Potsdam as Court Composer,
attempting to win him away from Your Majesty
and from London too
there came an extremely lucrative offer, which Mozart
rejected just as he had the Prussian.
At which my husband *knew* – although for a long time
he was no longer being betrayed, but informed by me,
he *must* have seen the truth:
that he had lost me for ever.
That a woman Mozart could not take with him,
in other words a married woman, kept him in Vienna,
where he was financially in an impossible situation…

LEOPOLD: (*Caught out, since that was exactly the situation.*)
Would that be any sort of complaint against us?

MAGDALENA: (*Unable to make any other sort of answer,
places the blame for Mozart's financial plight, for which
Vienna, if not the imperial house, was responsible, squarely to
Constanze's account.*)
By no means, Your Majesty, only here in Vienna
he was – it pains me to say it – he was
much put upon, financially, by his…what to call her?
By what is now his widow. She cannot be called his wife,
not for years now, since she has left him, and gone to Baden:
and her youngest child is by Mozart's pupil, Suessmayr,
as can be proved by Mozart's trip abroad.

It was important to her to restore Mozart's standing as a
father...
My pregnancy was no 'accident', as they say, it was
wanted...
by him and by me...but

*She is in tears again.*

what are men, that they should make plans.
Your Majesty just said it.

LEOPOLD: (*Not without irony.*)
And *your* husband – we sympathise with poor Hofdemel –
was he too kept from travel...because
you seemed so sure you were with child by Mozart?

MAGDALENA: (*Self-confidently.*)
The marriage between Hofdemel and me
no longer existed, Majesty.
The moment always comes sooner than one wants
when either distaste or pride prevent one from lying!
Perhaps because I had my own income,
earned as a pianist and teacher,
and my father in Bruenn supported me...

LEOPOLD: Your father is in the same trade, but with the
Church?

MAGDALENA: That is so, Majesty. His Excellency
the Archbishop's cathedral Kapellmeister in Bruenn.
Three months ago, on the way back from Prague,
where his opera 'Titus' had been performed in honour
of Your Majesty's enthronement as King of Bohemia,
Mozart visited my father. And spoke to him too
about his absolute certainty of death.
Probably because Constanze
had taken along her lover with her,
Suessmayr, father of her child –
what a humiliation for Mozart, that travelling companion –
he had had higher expenses than usual, and he borrowed

a very little money from my father,
and insisted on leaving his heavy gold watch as surety!
With the terrible reasoning:
'I know, Herr Pokorny, I shall never be able to pay this
back.'

LEOPOLD: (*As she fights with her tears.*)
Were you with Mozart in Prague and Bruenn?

MAGDALENA: (*Miserably.*)
How would I, how could I have, Majesty!
Please believe me, I was honestly intending
to separate from Hofdemel.
How often I *begged* him,
while we were still talking to each other,
to find someone else, and let me go.
I could not just leave, as Hofdemel
would have kept Theresa, our child, as hostage.
That I was pregnant made him mad, yes, bewitched.
He must have believed what he screamed at me at the end,
that he could not live with the child...of that other.
A child of Mozart's round him night and day
could not have been. I should never have told him.
That sent him mad, drove him to try to kill me,
and thinking I was dead – to suicide!
Who would cast the first stone!

*MAGDALENA has brought out this lie so convincingly, that
the Emperor almost believes – he is not sure himself how far
– that it is her confession, and not the murder of Mozart, that
drove Hofdemel to the attempt on her life.*

I feel so wretched, so guilty, in front of Hofdemel;
on the other side I am so calm, so proud,
that I could give Mozart his last happiness...
his high point of creativity.

LEOPOLD: Oh, yes –
'The Magic Flute', you are quite right, that is the highest!

MAGDALENA: Forgive me, Majesty, this intimacy,
      but since we are speaking of life and death:
      Mozart was nothing without his bed – and his wife knew it,
      but she still left him for
      the charming – young – and that was all he was –
      Suessmayr!
      Mozart was a lot more precisely convinced, more than
                                                we thought,
      more than we believed, of his approaching death.
      Without love he could have gone on living,
      many people must, but not composing, Majesty.
      I can hardly speak, forgive me, Your Majesty, when I think,
      when I see, always before my eyes, how often
      fits of tears would shake him, which were in fact
      a relief, a sort of salvation…
      If I was not with him, he could not,
      for fear of death, go on composing…
      What he wrote at the end is so divine,
      that's why I carry it with me all the time,
      my copy of the Requiem: I would read it in bed in
                                                hospital…

LEOPOLD: (*With the true curiosity of the passionate, educated,
      musician, picks up the copy from the spinet, where she had left
      her gift.*) True generosity,
      to have this copy made as a gift for us.

MAGDALENA: A wretched, messy copy only – Majesty,
      my notes are…if only I may beg Your Majesty's patience
      in the regulation of Mozart's financial affairs.
      His widow, as Your Majesty said at the start of this audience,
      had requested the first performance of the Requiem
      to settle the debts he left behind –
      and in the whole Residency the talk is of his supposed debts.
      But this is libellous, Majesty!
      I have already explained how Mozart in September
      had to ask my father for a very modest loan,
      which he only accepted if my father – much against his
                                                will –

would take Mozart's gold watch as guarantee.
He was always as correct as that, with money.
Hodfdemel too always got back with interest,
which he did not in the least want,
and on time, whatever Mozart borrowed from him!

LEOPOLD: (*Putting down the score, he had been reading,
impatiently, as she talked, since he is no longer interested.*)
Is it true – the widow Mozart told us yesterday,
without however, as she admitted, being precisely informed,
that the man who commissioned the Requiem paid cash,
so as to be able to perform it as his own composition?

MAGDALENA: It is true.
And he is not the first who wanted to issue Mozart's
music as his own!
It comes from the fact that of all his six hundred works,
hardly more than sixty have been printed!
That is why he gave me every sheet
of the requiem as he finished it to copy.
Because he realised, this was his last.
He was not in any financial need, but
he had to go along with the absurd demand of the man
who commissioned it. But that man,
who did not want to reveal his name
cannot have hoped Mozart would let it go
without taking a copy!
The whole mystery of the Requiem preoccupied Mozart
abnormally… I was with him once,
and actually saw the messenger…
A completely ordinary, insignificant man,
grey as a herring and about as thin,
speaking like an ostler or a groom,
but bringing a great deal of money.
Mozart's soaring, but at the time feverish imagination
could not see a perfectly ordinary messenger
of a client wishing to remain anonymous
in this more than ordinary man…oh, no!
In a panic he saw Death itself – how shall I put it –

in his earthly appearance.
You couldn't get it out of his head.

LEOPOLD: Now, my dear,
as far as his sad and all too early death
is concerned, he was not only not wrong,
but saw more realistically than all of us
how soon he would have to be going.
Would we not, should we not
and you must agree with this – let him lie,
not take this panic talk of poisoning seriously,
to be investigated post-mortem?
If the doctors say nothing, no doubt for a very good reason?

MAGDALENA: Since Majesty has been so good
to consult me in this matter, I say frankly: let it lie.
Majesty, there *cannot* have been anyone with a reason
to give Mozart poison!
Even my husband only discovered after Mozart had been
buried,
what was driving him mad! That I was with child again
and by whom!

LEOPOLD: (*interrupts impatiently.*)
Let us have no more repetition of this nonsense!

MAGDALENA: (*Now very much afraid the Emperor will have
Mozart exhumed, and realising nothing could set such a process
in motion so effectively as advising against it.*)
Should Majesty in any way entertain this suspicion
of poisoning, share it with Mozart himself,
then your Majesty must have him exhumed!

LEOPOLD: (*Sets this aside, almost with a laugh.*)
'Suspicion? – two doctors examined him!
Must have him exhumed? Happily no such thing.
we must avoid damage to the monarchy…
What sort of scandal would that be, to the civilised world,
what sort of hue and cry…if it came out
that even a Mozart could not be sure of his life

in our capital city of Vienna!
that is the only way, the only way, my dear Hofdemel,
that a city or an emperor can regard this misfortune.
The cloak of royalty has – how often –
to be the cloak which hides what must not be seen…
Sit down there, take a pen, and write,
here is some court paper

*He hands her a double sheet of luxurious writing-paper,
which she accepts with a curtsey.*

and then take it yourself to St Stephan's, to
his Imperial Highness the Archbishop.
Now let us work together to deceive the Cardinal of Vienna.

*He gives another of his characteristic short laughs.*

Music has brought us this far, that we have become
your accomplice, against our better knowledge or thinking!

*Another laugh.*

Very well then: We, Leopold, by the grace of God,
Emperor of the Holy Roman Empire, the German nation
                                                    and
King of Hungary – colon:
are you there? We are not going too fast for you?

MAGDALENA: (*Half-standing.*)
Very good, Your Majesty – my most humble thanks
for your Majesty's great honour… I can keep up all right.

LEOPOLD: (*Once more picks up the 'Requiem' from the spinet;
one can feel his passionate curiosity for new music. He reads
from the 'Requiem', then continues – with reluctance enough –
with his dictation.*)
As our brother in the Lord, we request Your Eminence
that Your Eminence should, as an Act of mercy,
in the Name of Christ, allow our Official of Justice Franz
                                                    Hofdemel
who had served us in duty and loyalty for two decades,

although deceased by reason of suicide,
to receive, with all blessings of the one True Church,
the honour of burial in consecrated ground,
as comfort for widow and child.
Since the – wait! Make a new paragraph,
two finger space.

MAGDALENA: (*Half rising.*)
Very good, Your Majesty: two finger space.

LEOPOLD: (*Continuing reflectively in time with his walk; at
one point – while thinking – he even takes MAGDALENA by
the shoulder.*)
Since...it has become a matter of knowledge of the
residence-city... no,
residence will be enough...knowledge of the residence...
Since the...don't mind about corrections – of the...what
did we say?

MAGDALENA: Since it has become a matter of knowledge
of the residence-city...no:
Of the residence was your Majesty's last word.

LEOPOLD: ...it has become a matter of knowledge to the
residence of the attempted murder of his wife by the
Senior Clerk of the Court of Justice, who was clearly and
suddenly deprived of his reason...will be placed in a
more disadvantageous light – which has also recently
been made manifest to us – by the fact that the woman in
question was with child, which Your Eminence, in
accordance with our most deeply-felt request, will treat
as confidential, so as to avoid adding to the gutter- and
street-gossip of Vienna. The woman, an admired pianist
under her father's name of Pokorny, has several times
been recommended to Your Eminence, who has indeed
heard her perform upon the great organ in Your
Eminence's own most Christian Cathedral, will – as she
has assured us in an audience, at the end of which we
have, for the sake of greater confidentiality, dictated this

our petition to Your Eminence to her – will be departing
for her native city of Bruenn, as soon as her unfortunate
husband, without any doubt deprived completely of his
reason, shall have been decently, and attended with no
diminution of the priestly blessings due to him, laid to
rest in the earth, which can only be brought about by our
trust in the contrivance of Your Eminence's often times
manifested goodness. Punktum and sandshaker. At long
last, a full stop.

MAGDALENA: Very good, Your Majesty, full stop:
  Majesty is too kind…

LEOPOLD: Are we so? Well – we are sick and tired of the
                                                    talk…
  And would also wish…

MAGDALENA: This, Majesty – am I to take this down?

LEOPOLD: (*With his short, characteristic laugh.*)
  God preserve us – no! Don't write it down!
  this is for your ear alone:
  We do not wish so honest and dutiful a servant
  as Hofdemel was to us for so many years,
  to be sewn into a cow-hide
  for the knacker's yard,
  merely because he, as a powerless nobody,
  wished to defend his man's honour
  against the most famous of all the subjects
  of us, or of our blessed mother Teresia, rest her soul,
  in a manner that…
  really, admittedly,
  could have been denounced as mentally ill.
  You yourself will now immediately take this petition,
  to His Grace the Archbishop…you are to hand it
  to His Grace in person. And to no one else!
  The Cardinal will admit you, as soon as you say
  you have come from the Emperor.

MAGDALENA: If Majesty will please to permit
    that I, with your Majesty's gracious permission,
    in Your Majesty's presence, may make a fair copy of
                                Your Majesty's dictation.

LEOPOLD: As you wish – meanwhile we will take a look
    at the Requiem, we are already eaten up with curiosity…

MAGDALENA: (*Rising and curtseying.*)
    The copy is not quite complete,
    as Mozart's widow did not allow me
    to see the last few pages
    for comparison with this version.

LEOPOLD: (*Laughs.*)
    Is that supposed to astonish us, Madame Hofdemel,
    that the affection between yourself and the widow Mozart
    is somewhat limited in its range?
    If Mozart got you with child…

MAGDALENA: After Suessmayr, in a year-long
    entanglement with Constanze, gave her,
    so we are told, her last child.

LEOPOLD: (*Throwing both arms in the air.*)
    Now let us not be burdened with stories of that kind!
    I dare say an Emperor hears gossip more eagerly
    than any of his servants,
    because he hears that sort of thing so seldom,
    though no one can find out more about people
    than through what they gossip about.
    Imagine, were an emperor to beat his head
    about the marital sideslips of his subjects…
    We look with indifference at who has whom! Main thing:
    breeding goes on and what it produces is healthy…
    Our late mother, though an obedient daughter of the Church,
    in startling contrast to her sixteen children –
    nevertheless, when she had to listen to scandal,
    always quoted two maxims of Marcus Aurelius:
    leave men alone with their sins, and
    always judge milder than the law prescribes.

MAGDALENA: (*Flattered at this intimacy of the Emperor's.*)
    All subjects of Her Majesty, the late Empress Maria Teresia
    and I was made aware of this even as a child! –
    owe her unexampled gratitude and devotion for that!

LEOPOLD: (*With the slight bitterness always felt when children
    talk about elders who were more important than they are.*)
    Yes, unexampled! Your word! It is not easy
    to be the mere imitator of great predecessors on a throne.
    When young, we all think we can do everything better
    than our elders. From fifty on we just hope
    to be able to do about as well as they did.
    Only the Church failed sufficiently to withstand that
                                            great woman,
    when she transported the Salzburg Protestants
    to the Banat in Hungary, and then as far as the Black Sea
    only allowing those most pitiable of creatures free passage
    at the appalling price of leaving their children behind,
    to be made future monks and nuns…crippled.
    Healthy beings who are not allowed to breed, are crippled.
    How much did Belief, whether heavenly or earthly,
    make any one infected with it worse
    than he was by nature. It was our brother Joseph
    first had to show that obstinacy, the only thing
    that can be used to defy the otherwise suffocating
                                            intolerance
    of the mighty Church to the good of the State!

MAGDALENA: (*Feeling that it benefits this Emperor, who has
    not yet distinguished himself by any particular achievement, if
    he can cite at least one fact that will reduce the importance of
    his mother and predecessor – and rightly condemn it, she
    quickly and cunningly seizes on the answer that LEOPOLD
    happily accepts.*)
    Your Majesty has just, several times, in your
    so gracious arrangement for my poor Hofdemel
    to the Cardinal of Vienna –

LEOPOLD: Which you will personally hand to His Eminence!

MAGDALENA: (*With a deep bow.*)
Personally hand to him, very good!
Your Majesty has proved what we subjects have long
been aware of in love and gratitude:
namely, how constantly Your Majesty has remained true
to the reforms of your Majesty's late departed brother
Joseph,
and defended them against all attempts
of the clergy to annul them.
That we here in Vienna need bow our heads
only to God and our beloved imperial house –
and to no other power – we thank Your Majesty alone,
since Your Majesty's late brother was so much too soon
taken from us,
before his decrees of tolerance
had achieved their final conclusive force.

LEOPOLD: Had we come to the end of our letter?

MAGDALENA: Your Majesty's final words were:
'only brought about by our trust in Your Eminence's so
often manifested goodness.'

LEOPOLD: (*With a movement of his hand, for her to sit as he
wishes to finish dictating.*)
We have no wish to lie, my dear Pokorny,
we shall write nothing but the truth, if not the whole...
well, then, add this:
Your Eminence will doubtless take the by no means
recent rumours concerning the irregularities of behaviour,
well-known to the Residence, of the late Mozart
*Ccum grano salis,* as Your Eminence will also understand
the statement, made in a state of mental disturbance,
by the Clerk of Justice Hofdemel, against his wife,
to justify his – well nigh successful – attempt on her life:
namely that Mozart should have been the father of the child
which she will – when do you expect it?

MAGDALENA: In five months time, Your Majesty.

LEOPOLD: Which she is expecting in five months time,
    comma, Your Eminence may judge appropriately,
    in other words, comma, relegate to the realm of madness,
    so that Eminence before God, with accompaniment
                                         spiritual
    and musical, may despatch the much to be pitied
    and self-slaughtered madman, on his way to eternity –
    Finish!
    No, not finish – but:
    To eternity,
    where Hofdemel will be expected by a judge
    whom no earthly office can anticipate, full stop.
    No, not full stop! But dash –
    thus we hope Your Eminence and ourselves
    to be of one mind, another dash –
    to anticipate which is within the authority
    of neither the secular nor the spiritual power.
    Your Eminence's most affectionate…
    Punctum and sander.

MAGDALENA: With Your Majesty's permission,
    that I should immediately make a fair copy here…

LEOPOLD: Yes, yes, yes – of course! Sit there, while we
    devote ourselves to Mozart's – how did he put it? –
    legacy, his 'Requiem',
    until we can finally sign what you have written!

*MAGDALENA places the 'Requiem' ready for him on the
spinet. The Emperor sits, and she opens the first page for him.
As he begins to play, she briskly takes a lighted spill from the
fireplace and lights the two candles on the spinet, curtseys,
and begins to make her fair copy.*

(*After two minutes or so.*) What a beginning! Delicious!

*Another two minutes and the curtain falls.*

*The End.*